THE THREAT OF RADICAL FUNDAMENTALISM

Priestcraft Revisited

By
Jack   Lasley

A NISGO Publication
P.O. Box 549
Cocoa, Florida 32923

NISGO Publications
P. O. Box 549
Cocoa, Florida 32923

Manufactured in the
United States of America

100 % recycled paper

The Author

Jack Lasley is the author of numerous articles on matters of international concern; founder of the Institute of International Studies at Chapel Hill, North Carolina; charter member of the World Law Center, and the American Freedom Association; former member of the National Panel of Arbitration of the American Arbitration Association. Member of the North Carolina Bar and Counselor of the Supreme Court of the United States.

He is the author of several books, among them: *The War System and You*, *My Country — Right or Wrong?*, *The Power Within*, and *Priestcraft and the Slaughterhouse Religion*.

Foreword

This book is about freedom — freedom to write, speak, read and view what one wishes; freedom from the officious intermeddling of church and state that would strip away these freedoms.

THE FUNDAMENTALIST THREAT

W e will examine excerpts from the writings of seven key players in the birth-drama of this nation.

The men we will consider comprise a highly select group in the sense that included is the author of the Declaration of Independence; the first Secretary of the Treasury; the presiding officer at the Constitutional Convention; the "Father of His Country"; the "Father of the Constitution"; our most illustrious diplomat, and the man whose writings are said to have begun the concerted movement in this country toward its independence. Among this select group are the first four presidents of the United States.

By any reasonable standard we have included those who played the most vital roles in shaping the attitudes of all involved in the birth of our nation.

These were reasoning, intelligent men who founded a country wherein ideas were to be freely held and expressed, particularly those regarding personal beliefs. Religion was to be free from state support; the people free from religious inquisitions and laws prescribing their peaceful religious conduct.

Revolutionaries

In our current anti-revolutionary fervor, we tend to forget that our nation's Founding Fathers were revolutionaries, who rejected

1

the fundamentalist's religious concept that mankind is depraved. They trusted the good sense of the common man and, using this as a base, built a nation that was — and is — the envy of the world.

In a misguided attempt to correct problems of national discontent, drug abuse, family dissolution, and a general disquiet, many have turned to the radical religious right in an effort to regain lost and treasured values. While most religion may be of great benefit, the religious right is steeped in bigotry. It threatens our educational system, and the freedoms that made this country great.

So long as these radicals rolled in the aisles and stayed in their churches, confining themselves to good works, they presented no immediate, pressing danger. Now they have become a national political force, and what many of them stand for, should be generally known. The incidious threat they present is the subject of the discussions that follow:

Understanding the Threat

Each march to freedom takes a different route. All seek deliverance from what Alexander Hamilton called "rein and spur." The protection of freedoms once acquired requires constant vigilance. Sometimes threats to our freedoms come from unsuspected and seemingly innocuous sources; this is the case with radical religious fundamentalism.

Because of its seductive, highly emotional, showbiz attractiveness, some people have lost a sense for the proper use of reason and are going off the deep end in a ecclesiastical binge. This dive into religious fanaticism is clearly within the rights of those who wish to take the plunge. It is also within the rights of those opposed to their ideas not to vote for their candidates for public office. As a political machine, the fanatical right, awash as it is in bigotry and ignorance, threatens our educational system, and the individual freedoms that made our country great.

As the people of the earth hunger for peace and food, religious fanaticism daily manifests itself throughout the world diverting minds and money from human needs. It is beginning to happen here, as abortion clinics are bombed, and in numerous other less violent ways, our freedoms come under attack.

The very extremist views that forced our forebears to seek a new nation on these shores are being resurrected in the name of patriotism and family values. The danger is that in our zeal to return to honorable standards of the past, we lose sight of the value we once placed on freedom and our ability to reason for ourselves.

Habits of critical thinking that caused men to question the divine right of kings, also caused our nation's Founding Fathers to question the doctrines of the church. They did not believe these doctrines to be sacrosanct. They dared to bring reason into play where faith had stood alone. Reason was not seen as anti-religious, but as supportive of genuine faith, albeit that faith was sometimes unorthodox.

Typically, the fanatic fundamentalist will see faith in an either/or frame: it is either good or bad; it's "us and them." To him, good faith is like his own; otherwise it's "cultish" in character. There is no room for academic disagreement, but deep-seated hostility for those who philosophically differ with him. The abortionist, pornographer, advocate of world government, supporter of the United Nations and equal rights for women and minority groups; those who advocate peace and oppose corporal and capital punishment, are all considered subversive, agents of the anti-Christ and — worst of all — "liberals."

How soon we forget that our nation's key Founding Fathers were revolutionaries and religious liberals. Yet none was without religious faith. All believed in God, but none covered here — as stated earlier — would qualify as a "full gospel, evangelical charismatic" fundamentalist. They agreed that all humans are endowed by their creator with certain natural rights; and, with the possible exception of Thomas Paine, they felt government should keep clear of religious

4

beliefs.[1] Believers and non-believers were to be equal citizens, free from governmental interference with their personal religious views and the public expression of those views. While these Founding Fathers were religious liberals and revolutionaries, they are often presented by the right as orthodox Christian conservatives. We shall see later what the Founding Fathers had to say about religion and religious freedom.

The Inquisition was fresh in their minds, as were the excesses of Christians in this country after it began to be settled. The Founding Fathers were not averse to commenting critically on certain religious institutions and practices which they called "popery"[2] and "priestcraft."[3] They believed that criticism of religion does not constitute bigotry. Quite the opposite. It is the bigot who opposes new ideas and critical thinking.

As our national debt soars into the trillions of dollars and we otherwise prostitute our resources in a futile attempt to secure our freedoms through armaments and more jails, we must not lose sight of a force within seeking to deprive us of our basic freedoms. This movement may be more fanatic and immediate than we realize, and is coming from a generally unsuspected source; i.e., the radical religious right, who claim to base their beliefs on the very words of God.

Salvation

While the Founding Fathers showed a common respect for the individual rights of all people, the religious fanatic is taught to "love the brethren and pray for the unsaved." If you argue from the Bible that it often seeks to direct its readers to have compassion and to love one's neighbors, whomever they might be,[4] you will get nowhere. Again, to these fundamentalists, it's us and them with "them" being the "unsaved," a term of opprobrium which applies to everyone — Catholics, Jews, even mainline Protestants _ who don't agree with their dogmas or otherwise fail to meet the fundamentalist's notions of one righteous before God.

If you are not "saved" and "filled with the Holy Ghost with evidence of speaking in tongues," the pentecostal charismatic will pray for you. You may be surprised to learn that the prayer being lifted up in your behalf is that you will be, if necessary, physically or fiscally stricken to such an extent that you will be driven to your knees, repent of your "sins," and be "saved." Glory!

Salvation in their frame of reference, sufficient to qualify a person as one of the "brethren," involves a certain ritual which generally follows this format: The guilt-ridden parishioner kneels at the altar accompanied by one or more certified believers. As they pray together, the one seeking to become one of the "brethren" is cajoled to "let it all out," or words to that effect. There may be prolonged moments of attempts to "get it all out." At this point a "catcher" quietly moves into the area. When babbling begins, the preacher is called over to listen and, in effect, to certify that the sounds being made are "genuine." You know the supplicant has been duly approved and "saved" when the preacher gives a bone dry chuckle and smiling parternalistically, lays hands on the supplicant. At this point the new brother or sister, having arisen momentarily, may keel over in a swoon, being careful to fall into the arms of the "catcher" who has been stratigically positioning himself to lower the supplicant — now "slain in the Spirit" — to the floor. On rising, the newly "saved" one is asked to testify. There usually follows a few tearful words of joy at having the burden of guilt lifted. (Building a sense of guilt and then providing relief through "salvation" drives the church and fills its collection plates.)

Feeling relieved of guilt, the newly "saved" brother or sister may for a week or so attend church, testify, and even come in off-hours to do chores around the church building. By this time the preacher is but a little lower than the Deity to the initiate, and the salvation process is now completed in the eyes of the congregation.

It is important to remember that even if one belongs to a mainline church, but has not followed the Spirit-filling, certifying process in a "full gospel, Bible-believing, pentecostal" church, his or her claim to salvation is at best suspect to most charismatic fundamentalists. Of course this whole procedure, while emotionally lifting and exciting, bears closer resemblance to a fraternity or social club initiation than to a voluntary, reflective, heartfelt and reasoned expression of belief arrived at over an extended period of time.

Most importantly, the seed is sown in the minds of the congregation that those who have not followed such a routine are not good — at least not complete — Christians. They may grudgingly say that some mainliners are "saved," but you wonder if they mean it. According to their beliefs, most people will eventually burn in hell because the Bible says, they remind you, that the gateway to heaven is narrow and few will enter.[5] This is in sharp contrast to the high value placed on all people by the Founding Fathers, and by Jesus, if one reads the entire Sermon on the Mount with an open mind.[6]

In addition to the self-exalting ritual of certifying salvation, the "full gospel, evangelical, charismatic," fundamentalist preacher is called upon to do the more mundane tasks of dedicating children, performing marriages, visiting the sick, and officiating at funerals. It's all very heady stuff, not well suited to genuine humility, but well suited to feigned piety and exhalted self-esteem. So don't let those false smiles, hand holdings, and hugs fool you. He may be a saint, but there's a chance that beneath that benign exterior may beat the heart of a mercenary, a charlatan, and a bigot.

Faith Healers

The manifest danger of the faith-healing fundamentalist preacher is that he may use his exhalted status to prey upon the emotional dependencies of his followers to their detriment. Delayed medical care can sometimes exacerbate an illness, even result in death. To the adoring parishioner, reliance on the healing hand of the Master, administered through one appearing to be a conduit for His power, can be irresistable. What would you do if faced with a seemingly no-win medical situation? You would probably grasp at anything that held the slightest ray of hope for the alleviation of your pain and suffering. What, then, could be more logical than to turn in your distress to the all-time winner. The "all powerful" One who cannot lose? Certainly this is the mindset encouraged by these preachers. The opportunity for fraud is evident. The likelihood of relatives and loved ones later being able to prove fraud, remote to nonexistent.

Suppose the sick person seeking relief gives or leaves all or a portion of his earthly wealth to the preacher or his church. The difficulty in having such a gift or bequest later set aside for fraud would be considerable. In the first place, there would be a natural reluctance by the decedent's heirs to sue a church or a "man of God." If such a suit were brought, the defendant could mount a multifaceted defense. After all, people do die. Also the person ministered to was probably certifiably seriously ill when the donation or bequest was made. It would be difficult to show he was not comforted in his last illness, possibly "saved." In the eyes of many jurors this would have more than compensated for the decedent's gifts to his pastor and church, salvation being "more precious than gold."[7] In addition, the preacher would likely have been circumspect in his relationship with the decedent. So there would probably be no tangible evidence of chicanery or fraud.

Deception and the Almighty's Dollar

Have you ever heard a religious broadcast in which the evangelist asked for a "contribution" or "love gift" of at least a minimal amount in order for his listeners to receive something? If not, you haven't been listening. A preacher might say he will send you his latest tape on, say, "How to Overcome Materialism" if you will send him a contribution of at least some given amount. Well, that's no contribution, it's an offer to sell and a sale if you send the stated amount. Whatever is sent in is called a "contribution" or gift by the preacher for tax purposes.

1 0

Misrepresentations of this kind are daily fare on radio and TV gospel shows.

Ironically, with the possible exception of hypocrisy, Jesus probably told more parables inveighing against the possession of riches than against any other sin.[8] For the preacher it then becomes necessary to soften and put a new twist on these words of the Lord; to tone them down, so as not to offend rich people who might be or become financial supporters. So the dogma now in the churches is that Jesus really didn't preach against having wealth, it is the misuse of one's dollars that gets one in trouble upstairs.

This interpretation of the Bible goes over big. So many dream of wealth and are delighted to hear the preacher say their hoard of riches is permissible. For those who have struck it rich, they may keep their money so long as they keep some of it going to the pastor and church — at least 10% — in a day in which our taxes and charitable contributions constitute "doing unto others" in a grand way, outside the church.

There is one small passage in the Bible, that amounts to no more than a passing greeting between friends, which is used in an attempt to show one and all that God really wants all Christians to have lots of money.[9] Since it suits their purpose, this greeting has been used as a deitific pronouncement of desire that all believers become materially prosperous.

It is reported that one TV evangelist, bent on sustaining his political power, was able to raise $1 million in one day. (Such reports are hard to verify, as responsible audits and church business have yet to be wed. They are not even courting.) Yet the time may come when we see one or more of these more successful money raisers listed among the *Fortune 500*. But no matter how much they get, they want more. They plead for money for all manner of causes. But the one that gets most attention, is their need to meet the costs of TV and raido time. Reliance on divine Providence to supply these needs has long since been abandoned as ineffective. In today's world, the beggers of the street have taken a backseat to the beggers of the airwaves.

The pentecostal holy roller is repeatedly told by his preacher that it is the sum total of all like-minded believers that constitutes the church of God. It is not the church building, they are told, but the body of believers that constitutes the "church." This doctrine holds until the money runs low and repairs or that new addition are needed. Then, miraculously, a transformation occurs. The church building becomes the "church" and the parishioners are told in no uncertain terms, to bring not only their tithes, but such additional amounts of money as "God might lay on your heart," into the storehouse. Smooth!

Showbiz Religion

No doubt this is the time when there has been a marriage of convenience between the entertainment business and the church. World class cynics delight the fundamentalists with their "conservative" radio and TV shows; and, never have so many leather-lunged preachers and their entourages been projected so far and to so many potential contributors — all in living color. The devotees of stomp and shout religion can sit at home and catch the latest show. There is no pressing need now to hit the sawdust trail in search of religious entertainment. It's right there in your living room. Tents are fading. The clamor now is to get on TV. Only then can one of these preachers feel he has arrived and is really "serving the Lord."

If the fundamentalist once eschewed the fleshly things of this earth, no more. For example, Paul's comments about the proper dress and conduct of women in church[10] has long since been inundated in a flood of baubles and beads. For pure theatre, these shows are hard to beat. The thirst of the faithful for entertainment appears unquenchable.

The Role of Women

You can talk about your men of Gideon, you can talk about your men of Saul, but don't dare mention women's rights in a fundamentalist church. No, sir! Women are not to be on the official board of the church, nor to give prayers in church; they are not to take up collection, or be ordained with the same powers as their male counterparts. To the religious bigot, equal rights for women is patently the work of satan. Women who head other nations or otherwise do what "men are supposed to do," according to fundamentalist traditions, are considered the work of the devil.

Women are permitted to speak only "in tongues" during regular services. Whereas the dismissal prayer is occasionally given by a male member, not so for women. Women are never asked to pray in an intelligible language during the regular service. This may be one reason most messages in tongues are given by women; it's the only way they can be heard during the regular service in a fundamentalist church. The irony is that in the very chapter of the Bible in which Paul discusses speaking in tongues, he also says "it is a shame for a woman to speak in church."[11] This failure by the fundamentalists to follow biblical directive does not seem to disturb the fundamentalists, so long as the women speak in tongues in the church. (Men practically never speak in tongues in a fundamentalist church.)

The Bible directs women to dress with "shamefacedness and sobriety,"[12] and not to wear "gold, pearls, or costly array."[13] They are told their husbands are "the glory and image of God,"[14] while they are "the glory of the man."[15] It's not hard to tell the Bible was written by men. If you wonder where male sexism has its foundation, look no farther. Just so there is no confusion on the point, the Bible states that women are to be in subjection to men and it tells the woman not to teach or to exercise authority over the man.[16]

With such unequivocal support from the biblical teachings of Paul and Peter, it is not difficult to understand the fundamentalist's attitude toward women. At the same time, for the independent thinker, applying John Adams' free inquiry philosophy to the Bible, these teachings are unjust and not in keeping with the overall spirit of Christianity. The Founding Fathers, as we shall see, were not reluctant to point out the fact that much of the Bible is "sublime" — but not all of it. Jefferson said that finding the good is often like hunting for "diamonds in a dunghill."[17] Mixing the free inquiry philosophy of Adams' with this Jeffersonian metaphor, it can be fairly concluded that on the subject of equal rights for women, the diamonds are on the ladies, not in the Word.

Education

Much of the failure of the fundamentalist church to interpret the Bible in the light of modern knowledge, lies in the lack of education of its clergy. A knowledge of the Bible is all that is required to go on TV,

15

pointer in hand, and lecture from charts and illustrations on scientific and historical subjects. It is appalling to see TV evangelists with only a few years of grammar school as an educational background, plus possibly some Bible college diploma, lecturing to millions. Some of these preachers are even called "doctor," indicating a sheepskin — very appropriate — from some Bible college, has been received. You would think they would be ashamed to attempt to teach, with no graduate training, the subjects on which they pontificate. But, lo, have no misgivings; they have read the book they claim contains the answers to all problems. In addition, they claim to have been "called of God," and to have special spiritual insights that transcend historical and scientific evidence which might conflict with their interpretation of the Bible or their personal revelations from on high.

Remember, too, these preachers know their denomination's dogmas. It would be dangerous for them to stray from the given line. Many a preacher has been defrocked after being found guilty of thinking for himself and beyond dogmas.

Their lack of training would not be so bad if they did as George Washington, and educated themselves. But these are one-bookers. For them the Bible contains all the answers to all questions. Then if you are convinced the Bible holds all the wisdom one will ever need, then you and I would probably also be willing to try our hand at lecturing on any subject without chagrin.

The average small church fundamentalist preacher, poorly educated, but surrounded by parishioners who feel he is their earthly contact with God, is understandably not wanting to get too far afield in his theological thinking. It might muddy the waters that brought him to where he is and cause him to lose a good thing. In what other line of work could he wear expensive suits, keep his hands clean, have one or more late model cars, live rent-free in a comfortable home paid for by others. Yes, it pays to be good. These pray-for-pay men — keep the women out, too much competition — find free trips, appearances on TV, and all that entertainment, plus a hall to lecture in to their heart's content, just too much to jeopardize with unorthodoxy and reason.

To watch a charismatic preacher prance and stomp you would certainly think he had much in common with rock stars of the day; but, rock music is another item on their list of things demonic. It seems someone decided to fix a rock record so that if you played it backwards and listened carefully you might be able to hear something resembling the word "satan." That did it! From that critical moment in the history of the fundamentalist church, rockers and rock music have been off-limits, unless the words have a "Christian theme." The intrinsic musical quality of a particular piece of music is, of course, never involved in these judgments.

The quintessence of a successful devil-beating get-together consists of having a standing room only crowd; and, as the main attraction, a repentant rock and roller. His testimony as to the evils of rock music will turn the crowd on by confirming their opinions of this modern sound, along with their feelings of self-righteousness.

Had any good bonfires lately? Just wait till you are the first on your block to burn rock records! If you could have a performance like the one just described followed by a rock record burning, just think of the crowd you could raise. Think of the full collection plates; and, to top it all off, somebody just might get "saved." To insure success you might consider a porn-burn at the same time. Yes, bring those dirty books and magazines. Pitch in. First thing you know you will have old satan on the run.

You will, of course, want to gain publicity for your event by getting the community into the act. Have a committee scan the shelves of the school library for books with racy, cultish, or satanic themes. Don't forget to appoint another committee to picket the local mom and pop convenience store because they carry one or more girlie magazines. This should insure at least newspaper coverage.

Yes, even though the Judeo-Christian tradition is obsessed with circumcision and virginity, all sexy writings should certainly be consigned to the flames along with those rock records. Oops, and don't forget those books on evolution. Glory how they burn. You might even get the event carried on TV!

But wait. Are certain kinds of music and sex sinful? Since neither Jesus nor the devil left any writings, we will just have to take the word of those who claimed (and claim) to know God's opinions on these subjects; and, what more convenient authority than your own fundamentalist preacher?

Now hold on here another minute. Weren't these same churches against American jazz at its inception? Could it have been because jazz was conceived in the brothels of New Orleans and the speakeasys of Chicago? Is jazz not now generally considered one of our nation's truly native art forms? A problem then arises. Just suppose the local purifier of our thoughts, viewing and listening habits, discovers that Mozart had pre-marital sex. Hold on tight to those classical records, they might be next on the wax-to-burn hit parade. And suppose — just suppose — somebody had the nerve to point out to them the erotica in the Bible. What? You mean you haven't read the Song of Solomon? For shame! Can't you just imagine how all this mind purging would set with the Founding Fathers? We will get to that later.

The Bible

All this may seem far afield from the life of Jesus which so concerned the Founding Fathers, particularly Jefferson. Ostensibly, today's religious fanatics are in business to promote Bible-based Christianity. It then behooves us to take a look at the Word.

When stripped of its patina of supposed Deitistic endorsement, reason suggests that the writers of the Bible were just plain people. No claim is made within its covers to the effect that any of its authors were divine. Interestingly, some of its stories emphasize this point. Cornelius tried to worship the man we now call "Saint Peter" whose reaction was: "Stand up, I myself also am a man."[18] "Saint Paul" said essentially the same thing to the people of Lystra when they tried to treat him as a god.[19] Yet Peter and Paul, whose combined writings make up over half of the New Testament, are quoted from pulpits as if these men were what they said they were not; i.e., devine.

In fact all the books of the Bible were written by men. It was not lowered from heaven on a string; but written by perfectly ordinary people whose powers of memory and observations varied. There is no statement in the Bible that Paul ever saw Jesus in the flesh. It is also true that not one single word of either the New or the Old Testament has been found in its original manuscript. What we have are copies of

20

copies of the books of the Bible. During a period of more than two thousand years, until the printing press was developed, each succeeding rendition of these writings was laboriously copied by hand, usually by an adoring scribe whose desire to harmonize and embellish the text must have been compelling.

As we shall see, no one admired the philosophy of Jesus more than Jefferson; yet he, and others among the Founding Fathers, realized the true nature of the Bible, both its strengths and its weaknesses.

The principal dogma of the fundamentalist is that the Bible is the inerrant, infallible word of God containing no contradictions. Yet among those who founded our nation were several dissenters from this dogma. They knew the Bible was a rich storehouse of stories and philosophy. They also felt, as we shall see, that to believe all its stories was to confuse fact with fiction, history with lyric poetry.

A careful study of the Bible reveals contradictions, and errors too numerous to go into here. Such studies have been made not only by some of the Founding Fathers; but by many others in search of the historic Jesus.[20] It should appeal to reason that were the Old Testament complete, sufficient, and without error, there would be no need for a New Testament. For example, in the Book of Leviticus paragraph after paragraph in

21

chapter eleven details the creatures that are not to be eaten. In the New Testament, however, God tells Peter that all manner of four footed beasts, and creeping things, and fowls of the air may be eaten.[21]

The fundamentalists are caught in an embarrassing situation. Their dogma that the Bible is infallible and inerrant, containing the answers to all of mankinds problems, is patently false. Their own actions, of course, belie such professed belief. When they are struck with illness, they both read the Bible and seek medical attention. This well illustrates the fact that pragmatically man's existence has two components: the physical and the spiritual. It is a mistake to lump our existence into either.

The fundamentalists get into difficulty when they confuse the two. They cite Isaiah "with his stripes we are healed" and claim that healing was provided in the Atonement.[22] They preach that it is not God's will that any believers be sick. Since believers and non-believers get sick and die in about equal proportion, these fundamentalists have either misunderstood the Bible or God has lost control.

The Bible is an anthology of stories, fables, philosophy, and poetry. Only in the sense that all things come from God can it be said that the Bible is the "word of God." But repeated often enough and solemnized by ecclesiastical councils, the idea that the Bible somehow was divinely authored becomes accepted without question; a doctrine that becomes a given, except to those of reasoning minds. In truth, the dogma was created by - to use the Jeffersonian term — "priestcraft."[23] In writing to his nephew, Jefferson reminded the lad that religion is too important a matter not to investigate throughly.[24] Jefferson's own investigations proved to him that there is much in the Bible that lacks truth and inspiration.[25]

It should be noted, too, that some of the Bible's chief luminaries, including some of its principal authors, failed to lead exemplary lives. Moses is credited with writing the first five books of the Old Testament; David most of the Psalms; and Paul is believed to have authored over half the New Testament. Each was involed in killing and lesser transgressions according to the Bible.[26] So when we sit in reverential silence Sunday mornings listening to what they wrote, we might just remember the true source of the words we hear. If we believe we are hearing the words of God from a man of God, we just might be wrong on both counts.

An objective reading of the Bible and its history is threatening to the fundamentalist. Turn through its pages. See if you can find a good piece against slavery or racial prejudice. Are you happy with the Bible's handling of the matter of equal rights for women? Do you feel the treatment of leprosy outlined in

23

Leviticus[27] represents the medical treatment you would wish to receive if you were infected with this disease?

Manifestly, the Bible contains many beautifully expressive passages and well-told stories. But to use it to prove historic or scientific facts, or as a foretelling of our destiny, is subject to reasonable questioning considering the source of these writings. Should we, just to illustrate the point, consider it holy writ that the "elements shall melt with fervent heat, and the earth also and the works that are therein shall be burned up"?[28] That is what Peter wrote. Shall we sit idly by as the atrocities described in the book of Revelation occur?[29]

Because of these and other statements in the Bible, fundamentalists apparently feel a nuclear holocaust is inevitable, even welcome if it will usher in the return of Jesus Christ. What blasphemies they entertain in the name of piety! It could be argued that a just God would not preordain the destruction of the earth and its people. Thus to refrain from the use of law, order, and world government to better our lives and prevent nuclear disaster, because of the writings of men who lived hundreds of years ago, is not only not according to holy writ, but is nonsense in the extreme.

If we grant, for the sake of argument, that all those who wrote the Bible were inspired by God, does it make sense to also say that no other men have been so inspired? By what authority shall we exclude Mohammed and others who claimed to have received messages from God? Shall we prove the exclusiveness of the Bible by quoting the Bible? This is poor quality evidence of devine inspiration, to put it mildly.

Let us then think for ourselves, using our God-given reason which is our best shield against those who would use the Bible to mount self-righteous crusades to destroy our freedoms. Commenting on how the spirit of Jesus has been corrupted by priestcraft, Jefferson wrote: "before his [Jesus'] principles were departed from by those who professed to be his special servants, and perverted into an engine for enslaving mankind, and aggrandizing their oppressors . . . the purest system of morals ever before preached to man has been adulterated and sophisticated by artificial constructions, into a mere contrivance to filch wealth and power to themselves . . . "[30] Still we can be encouraged by the predictions of Jefferson that the genuine doctrines of Jesus, "so long perverted by his pseudopriests, will again be restored to their original purity" and that "this reformation will advance with the other improvements of the human mind."[31]

Love of God?

We are commanded by Jesus to love God with all our heart, soul, and mind.[32] From

Thomas Paine to Thomas Jefferson we will cover the spectrum of various religious beliefs of the Christians and Deists that brought our nation into being. As with Job of the Old Testament, they all seemed to have respected the awesome power of the force that rules the universe. But unlike the charismatic fundamentalists, they were not of a fawning obsequious bent. We will read later of Jefferson's observations regarding a Richmond, Virginia church in which, he observed, were held "meetings and praying parties" where the participants poured forth "the effusions of their love of Jesus in terms as amatory and carnal, as their modesty would permit them to use to a mere earthly lover."[33] He also objected to what he called the fear in religion "under which weak minds are serviley crouched."[34]

As the Christian passes through this life he watches his own body deteriorate and life about him recycled into new forms of matter. He takes solice in the biblical promise that there is a spirit world in the hereafter where all will be righted, and justice and mercy will be the rule. In this Christian heaven there will be no more sorrow, pain, and suffering. To paraphrase the old hymn, after one has been there ten thousand years, it will all have just begun.

Still, if this life is any indication of the measure of justice and mercy we are to receive in heaven, we have cause for concern.

Our celebrations on earth of the love of God may not only be premature but overdone, if we rely on empirical and biblical evidence only.

Thomas Paine was offended by talk of God as a destroyer and unjust judge. Probably most of the other Founding Fathers would have been similarly put off by such a portrayal of the Deity. But using the "reason" that Paine so admired, let us consider the evidence.

What force or power is accountable for the natural disasters that cause us such distress? Shall we put the blame on the devil and thereby create another god to join the Trinity? If we do, we sink ever deeper into the multi-god, Hellenistic-type quagmire Jefferson and Adams warned against.[35] Let us continue our investigation of the empirical and biblical evidence.

If you were God, would you:

1. Create the devil?[36]
2. Kill everyone on earth except eight persons?[37]
3 Plan, and allow to be carried out, the killing of Jesus Christ?[38]
4. Create all the germs, viruses, mutant genes, and other agents that have plagued all creatures since life began?[39]
5. Allow babies to be born deformed?[40]
6. Have women ravished and children "dashed to pieces" before their parents?[41]

7. Permit entire open cities to be destroyed by fire, bombardment or other calamity?[42]

8. Cause the sins of the fathers to be visited on the children to the third and fourth generations?[43]

9. Plan the violence and destruction described in the book of Revelation?[44]

10. Destroy the earth and its elements by fire?[45]

This is the God of the fundamentalist. For the theologist, moralist, sociologist, ecologist, and all those engaged in life sciences, ethics, and for Christians generally, these Bible-based attributions to God are difficult to avoid and troublesome.

Our efforts on earth are deemed "good" when we perform useful, constructive work, and do what we can to ease suffering, and prevent death and destruction. We even extend these efforts to animals.

Beached whales are taken to marine biological facilities for treatment and subsequent release. Creatures of all kinds are taken to shelters or sanctuaries when found sick or wounded. It is our nature to fight nature and not let it run its course in such cases. We create endangered species lists and consider heroes those who find vaccines and other means to destroy the deforming and deadly agents of nature that threaten man and beast.

Nature is truly bloody in tooth and claw. Nothing walks, crawls, or swims that does not have a myriad agents set to attack its body. Those who wrote the Bible thought of them as evil spirits, demons, or agents of satan. We know them to be a material part of the structure that has been with us since early in the creation process. The advent of the microscope and the advance of science generally have given us new insights into the previously unseen microscopic world of genes, genetic constructions, germs, and viruses. It is now evident that such forces of destruction are part of the warp and woof of creation affecting both "good" and "bad" people and other creatures with essentially equal randomness. The latest serums and medical techniques have replaced the mud and spittle of Bible days.[46] Still the agents of destruction wear us down and are more than enough to cause the ordnary human being to cry out in his anguish — as did David and Jesus — "my God, my God, why hast thou forsaken me?"[47]

There are indeed those times when we are so threatened by infirmities that we turn in our desperation to those who can give us spiritual solace. At such times our reason is so encumbered with anxiety that we are far from being free agents, or objective thinkers. When a person feels death clutching at his vitals, in this stricken condition, he naturally turns to any that might ameliorate — if not cure — his condition.

At these times it can certainly do no harm to seek a boon from the Maker of heaven and earth by the nearest available route. Obviously such petitions are not always granted. However, even if such a beneficent dispensation is forthcoming, it patently does not relieve the injustices in the system borne by others who continue to suffer. The engines of pain and despair are endemic, profuse, and essentially random, and it does not lessen the unjust character of the creation if the Maker occasionally relieves a few of these pains. What of those who have lived exemplary lives yet die after suffering great pain and disability? To use the biblical story of Adam and Eve and "original sin" to justify these inequities, does little to support the good-God hypothesis.

It is at times when our emotions are unfettered; when our minds are clearest and most objective, that we can conclude there is much injustice built into the universe — when viewed with a reasoning perspective. If we abandon this keystone of our rational thought and moral code, we begin to construct a double standard: One for people, and another for God. Soon we begin to justify all manner of human calamities, accidents, and disorders in general, on the basis that God knows best. The child born deformed, or who dies from one of the multitude of microscopic organisms injected into the world, has clearly not been protected by an "all-good" creator.

Still this concept of an all-good God is basic to fundamentalism. If there is a good God, surely It would admire that believer who is honest in his emotional relationships; one who is not hypocritical in his feelings toward mankind and God. From Abraham to Jesus and including Moses, the men of the Bible were usually honest with God. When they objected to what was going on, they said so; yet, today's effusive in-church statements of love for God are never supplemented with sincere objections to the unjust way many just people suffer because of the very nature of the creation. Such statements would be considered shocking, even blasphemous.

Hypocrisy, which Jesus so vehemently opposed, is alive and well in the churches of the land. It is time we became honest with God. Praise him for the good things, and let him know when we feel injustice has been, or is being done, regardless of the source. Fakery before God fools no one but ourselves and those who have surrendered their reason. If there is an all-good God, the empirical evidence shows there cannot be an all-powerful God, as the inequities of this life are simply too great and numerous to support the validity of such a dual hypothesis.

Is God Good?

We tend to define what is "good" on the basis of human interrelatednesses and feelings, judging all happenings by the

31

Bentham pleasure/pain calculus. Getting outside this human-oriented perspective may be difficult, but it can bring a new and important quotient into our conception of "goodness." By being all-encompassing in our definition, we extend our view beyond human feelings to bring in the entire universe. Now "good" takes on new meaning. It becomes that which contributes to the regeneration and ongoing of the universe . . . that which makes it tick, as it were.

John Adams touched on this. He wrote: "The Creator looked into the remotest futurity, and saw his great designs accomplished by this inextricable, this mysterious complication of causes. But to rise still higher, this solar system is but one very small wheel in the great, the astonishing machine of the world. These stars, that twinkle in the heavens, have each of them a choir of planets, comets, and satellites, dancing round them, playing mutually on each other, and all, together, playing on the other systems that lie around them.

"Our system, considered as one body hanging on its center of gravity, may affect and be affected by all the other systems within the compass of creation. Thus it is highly probable every particle of matter influences and is influenced by every other particle in the whole collected universe."[48]

Thus there is no way a created being can escape playing out its role in the universal plan. No particular species fares any better than any other in the long run. Each has its life cycle and role to play. Each its own joys and terrors. No evidence supports the claim that man's existence in the overall spread of life on earth is in any special position as to equity, justice and mercy vis-a-vis the creation. We are not necessarily rewarded for goodness and punished for evil-doing; and, even though we seek to impose this standard on our existence, it is not the natural way the system operates.

Each creature, no matter how it acts in this life, inescapably contributes to the smooth functioning of the whole system. It is this interrelatedness — this service, if you will — to the entire creation that may win for each an equal position in the hereafter. Since ostensibly this "service" complies with the ineluctable intent of the Creator, each life should share equally with its own kind in heaven.

In this context, what individual creatures do during their lives and the length of their lives and experiences they encounter may be, in varying degrees, important to them and others, but makes no difference in the continuation of the integrated whole. It is not that the individual creature makes no difference, it is that what it does is unimportant to this overall eternal enterprise and oneness. An individual life may be good, or bad by our social standards; it may end early or reach extended years; it may reproduce its kind or not; its species may become extinct. Worlds may crumble, but others will take their places; matter is being recycled in the eternal process of renewal which remains as inviolable as it has been since the creation.

Thus unavoidably the role of the individual creature is played out as a temporary repository of atomic materials. At the death of the individual, this matter is liberated to find its way again into another combination of particles in the vast storehouse of matter that continues to act and react, assemble and disassemble. Only the **whole** is perfect. We unwittingly serve this whole integrated perfection by our very existence. Therefore, all participants in this material perfection serve it, and since their actions do not jeopardize its functioning no matter what they do, they are then "good" in this sense and serve the Maker of the system of perfection as a part thereof. Thus viewed, the Author of the universe can be seen as the Creator of a perfectly functioning universal machine of which all creatures are a salutary part.

The time we spend in directing others in what they should do — as if their eternal existence depended on what we deem to be good among men — may have no bearing on their eternal existence. It could well be that goodness of this kind interests the Creator not one iota. Goodness in the universal sense is insured and it is inviolable *ab initio*. The spiritual, everlasting reward of all creatures may not be dependent on what Jefferson called the "formulations of men," but guaranteed by the Creator to all Its creatures because they have played their part in the organized, integrated, ongoing whole of creation. No creature would be swept into eternal flames because of inherent weakness.

The fundamentalist's dogma that the great preponderance of people will not be "saved," but will burn in everlasting hell, does little to enhance the "good-God" doctrine. After all, no one asked to be created. We are imperfect products by design of the Creator, involuntarily here, proceeding through the overall perfectly functioning creation filled with destructive elements including mutant genes, germs, natural disasters and other destructive elements sewn into the universe. So viewed God has not lost control, but is supremely in command. Pain and suffering become morally irrelevant from the standpoint of this universal "goodness."

But in this analysis, we have strayed far afield from the ordinary concepts of right and wrong, good and evil, and have developed, like Saint Paul and other religionists, a man-made, rhetorical formulations, designed to convince our minds that God is good. Unlike fundamentalist dogma, it has the advantage of seeing all people not as depraved, but as eminently worthy sons and daughters of God, bound for heaven, no matter what form of mischief their uniqueness, individualism, and imperfections get them into.

We then conclude, as did Job of old, that God is fearsome, full of wonders, and awe inspiring, but these are not synonyms or euphemisms for goodness. Only in a highly structured, arcane sense, and within the hypothesis that omits most of the usual human norms of good and evil, can God be said to be "good."

Bigotry

During the '60's much attention was directed — and rightly so — toward racial bigots in our midst, some of whom traditionally wore sheets and hoods and burned crosses. We have always had those who were prejudiced against blacks, whites, Jews, Catholics, women, and so on. Their political clout was localized to non-existent.

Now we have among us those who have many of these same characteristics. Behind their amicable facade often hides a bigotry that far surpasses that of traditional racial or creedal hatreds. Within their acknowledged good qualities is a doctrine to the effect that all who are not "saved" — according to their definition of that term — will not go to heaven, but spend eternity in hell by edict of God. Those they deem unworthy to be with God in the hereafter even include mainline

36

Protestants who — in the fundamentalist's view — have not fully accepted Jesus as their personal savior, been filled with the Holy Ghost "with evidence of speaking in tongues," and baptised in water.

Of course this excludes not only most Americans but most of the people of the earth. One cleric is reported to have estimated that if everyone were to die at the same time, "80 to 90 percent" would "wind up in hell."

Remember, it is the duty of the fundamentalist to obey the Great Commmission of Jesus and to directly or indirectly take the gospel to all the world.[49] It is an extremely important element of their religion. Since the advent of TV and the rise of the shout and stomp, entertainment-oriented evangelist as a political phenomenon, a serious problem has arisen which deserves the careful consideration of the entire nation. Suppose, for example, we were to elect one of these religious bigots as president of the United States. Whom would he appoint to his cabinet or whom would he nominate for the Supreme Court? Would not ambassadors be selected with an eye toward carrying out the Great Commission of Jesus' to take the gospel to all the world?[50] If we add to the mix a Congress made up largely of fundamentalists, confirmation of presidential appointments would be almost a certainty.

Lest we forget, the "unsaved" comprise most people. Among them are the Jews,

Muslims, and even most professing Christians.[51] According to fundamentalist doctrine, God will deny entry into heaven to the "unsaved," and they are to spend eternity in hell; so clearly no God-fearing fundamentalist would appoint to high office one whom God had decreed to be bound for eternal flames. Thus the list of potential presidential appointees would soon dwindle down to a precious few. Can you imagine a Supreme Court packed with religious radicals? Heaven forbid!

This potential for ineptness in high places is not as far fetched as it might have been in the past. The juxtapostion of the advent of TV and a desire at all costs to get back to our basic standards, has sent us scurrying off to find these lost values among the most bigoted group the nation has ever spawned and their conservative supporters. We must not forget that pluralism is the key ongoing factor in the greatness of America.

We have made great strides in our attempts to rid our nation of the prejudices that may have denied Al Smith and Adlai Stevenson the presidency, and that today impedes the progress of women and certain minorities in their efforts to attain public office. Such prejudices should not be allowed to keep fundamentalists from public office if they can lay aside their bigotry for the good of the country. Yet the views of the radical right are so bizarre,[52] their committment to the denial of personal freedoms so deep seated, that the electorate can ingnore them only at its peril. To illustrate, under fundamentalist doctrine it is considered high sin to change one word of the Bible. Since Benjamin Franklin edited the Lord's Prayer;[53] and, Thomas Jefferson edited the New Testament,[54] these Founding Fathers would not be considered fit to hold public office under a present-day radical fundamentalist regime. And can you imagine fundamentalist support for John Adams or Thomas Paine, if they were living today? Details later.

Future political campaigns of the religious right will probably be run under the guise of restoring America's lost values. Sounds good and would certainly have wide voter appeal. But before you cast your ballot for a fundamentalist candidate, find out what he means by such terms as "like precious faith," "the brethern," and the big one, "salvation." Be careful, you may be voting for a bigoted, censorship minded, freedom destroying, military oriented elite group that could turn our nation from a democracy into a theocracy in short order. It has happed elsewhere. It must not happen here.

By the way, have you seen a fundamentalist youth corps arrayed in quasi-military uniforms, marching down the aisles of your local fundamentalist church? Believe me, you don't want to. It's a shocking sight.

The quick-draw attitude that has gotten our nation into such difficulties abroad, is right in line with fundamentalist philosophy. Their attitude towards violence, keeps them from touching the Sermon on the Mount except lightly and in passing. Whipping children, support for corporal and capital punishment, militarism, the denial of the principals of basic human equality, and a failure to acknowledge minority and women's rights, are all part and parcel of their philosophy. These positions they believe to be God-ordained and proper to the eternal order of things.

It would be not only ironic but tragic if in the name of Christianity we should lose our freedoms to religious radicals who claim to be the bearers of God's will for us, our nation, and its future.

Notes

1. Norman Cousins, *In God We Trust*, (New York: Harper & Brothers, 1958), pp. 417-423. Jack Lasley, *Priestcraft and the Slaughterhouse Religion*, NISGO Publications, 1987, pp. 90-92. Compare Jefferson's notes on the *Act for Religious Freedom*, Cousins, supra, pp. 121-127.

2. John Adams, *A Dissertation on the Canon and Feudal Law*, Boston Gazette, August, 1765. Cousins, supra, pp. 84-86.

3. Thomas Jefferson's letter to Joseph Priestley, March 21, 1801. Cousins, supra. pp. 130-131. Lasley, supra, p. 15 and p. 109.

4. Matthew 5:43-45; 19:19; 22:39; Romans 3:22; 10:12; Ephesians 4:4-6; First Timothy 2:5.

5. Matthew 7:13-14; Luke 13:24.

6. Matthew chapters 5, 6, and 7.

7, First Peter 1:7.

8. Matthew 13:22; 19:23-24; Mark 4:19; 10:25; Luke 6:24; 8:14; 12:16-21; 14:12-14; 16:1-13; 19-24; 18:18-25; 21:1-3. Second Corinthians 8:9.

9. Third John 2.

10. First Timothy 2:9.

11. First Corinthians 14:35.

12. Supra, note 10.

13. Supra.

14. First Corinthians 11:7.

15. Supra, note 14.

16. First Timothy 2:12.

17. Jefferson's letter to F.A. Van Der Kemp, April 25, 1816. Cousins, supra, pp. 172-173.

18. Acts 10:25-16.

19. Acts 14:8-15.

20. See: Jack Lasley, *Bible Errors and Contradictions, A Perspective*, NISGO Publications, 1982. Jack Lasley, *The Power Within*, NISGO Publications, 1984, et al.

21. Acts 11:3-9.

22. First Peter 2:24. See: Isaiah 53-5, et al.

23. Supra, note 3.

24. Jefferson's letter to his nephew, Peter Carr, August 10, 1787. Cousins, supra, pp. 127-129. Lasley, supra, note 1, pp. 57-59.

25. Supra, notes 1, 3, 17, 20 and 24.

26. Exodus 2:11-14; First Samuel 18:6-8; Acts 7:57-59, et al.

27. Leviticus chapters 13 and 14.

28. Second Peter 3:10-12.

29. Revelation chapters 14-19, et al.

30. Jefferson's letter to Samuel Kercheval, January 19, 1810. Cousins, supra, pp. 139-140. Lasley, supra, note 1, p. 61.

31. Jefferson's letter to Jared Sparks, November 4, 1820. Cousins, supra, p. 156.

32. Matthew 22:37; Mark 12:30.

33. Jefferson's letter to Thomas Cooper, November 2, 1822. Cousins, pp. 163-164.

34. Supra, note 24.

35. Jefferson's letter to Benjamin Waterhouse, June 26, 1822. Cousins, supra, pp. 160-161. Lasley, supra, note 1, pp. 69-70 and 71-74. See also: John Adams' letter to Jefferson, December 25, 1813. Cousins, supra, pp. 253-257.

36. Revelation 12:9; 12:12; 13:1-18; Isaiah 14:12; Luke 10:18; Colossians 1:16; John 1:3; Ephesians 3:9; re. all things made by God.

37. Genesis 6:7; 7:1-24; 8:1-22; 9:1-17.

38. Isaiah 53:12; Matthew 20:18-19; 26:54-56; 27:35; Mark 14:36; 14:49; 15:28; Luke 22:37; 24:25-27; 24:44; 24:46; John 3:16; 18:11 18:32; 19:36-37; Acts 17:3; Hebrews 11:17; James 2:21; First John 4:9.

39. John 1:3; Ephesians 3:9; Colossians 1:16.

40. Matthew 19:26; Mark 10:27; 14:36.

41. Psalms 137:9; Isaiah 13:16-18.

42. Supra, note 28.

43. Exodus 34:7; Numbers 14:18; Deuteronomy 5:9.

44. Revelation 6:8-17; 8:7-13; 9:15-19; 11:6-18; 14:10-20; 16:1-21; 17:16; 18:8-9; 19:11-21; et al.

45. Second Peter 3:10; Matthew 24:35; Luke 21:33.

46. Mark 7:32-36; 8:22-25; John 9:6-7.

47. Matthew 27:46; Mark 15:34.

48. Cousins, supra, pp. 83-84. Lasley, supra, note 1. p. 56. From Adams' diary, May 1, 1756.

49. Matthew 28:19-20; Mark 16:15; Luke 24:47.

50. Supra.

51. Ginny Graybiel, *Priest Defends Killing of Abortion Doctors*, Florida Today, January 12, 1995.

52. Supra.

53. Cousins, supra, pp. 21-23. Lasley, supra, note 1, p. 41.

54. Cousins, supra, pp. 173-216. See: Jefferson's letter to Charles Thomson, January 9, 1816. Cousins, supra, 145-146. Lasley, supra, note 1, pp. 62-63.

SEX AND RELIGION

Female Circumcision

The practice of female genital mutilation, sometimes called "female circumcision," has both ethnic and religious roots. One Islamic teacher is quoted as saying the practice is common in certain regions in order that "our women" (Muslim) will not "misbehave."[1]

A proposal of Dr. Obed Asamoah, acting minister of justice and attorney general of Ghana, mandated a three year prison term for "whoever excises, infibulates or otherwise mutilates the whole or any part of the labia minora, labia majora and the clitoris of another person."[2]

Dr. Asamoah points to a recent study which states that female genital mutilation is a health hazard affecting "every part of the victim's life." The harmful effects, the study reveals, "may occur at consumation of marriage, at delivery of the first child, or may be post-natal."[3]

Dr. A. A. Afrifa, psychologist, believes the practice should be eliminated "forever" in order to save "young girls the pain and trauma of going through such harrowing experiences."[4]

Female genital mutilation (FGM) is not only practiced in Africa but, according to the World Health Organization, approximately 90 million women worldwide have been subjected to FGM; and, that approximately 10,000 children are at risk in Britian alone.[5]

The World Health Organization, United Nations Human Rights Commission, and UNICEF have all issued declarations to the effect that female genital mutilation should be stopped.[6] It will be a formidable task since FGM is presently practiced in over 30 countries, according to the World Medical Association.[7]

The Bible's Fascination with Sex

Generally speaking, one is not identified today by the condition of his or her sexual parts. Yet the Bible is fascinated with such indentification. In biblical book after book reference is made to those who were "virgins."[8] The Bible also places great emphasis on circumcision. God made a covenant with Abraham concerning his penis and Abraham was then circumcised as a "token of the covenant betwixt me and you."[9] Also in the covenant was the promise that each male child born thereafter would be circumcised.[10]

Virility also seemed to have facinated the writers of the first few books of the Bible. Adam, Noah, Seth, Enos, and Methuselah, et al., each not only lived to be over 900 years old but are said, at 90 years of age and older, to have sired children.[11] For example, Seth had a child at age 105 and, at the age of 187, Methuselah fathered Lamech.[12] The ladies also apparently had strong reproductive powers, as Abraham's wife had Isaac when she was 90 years old.[13]

The Song of Solomon in the Old Testament is sexually explicit. Portions of that biblical book will illustrate the point:

"How beautiful are thy feet with shoes, O prince's daughter! The joints of thy thighs are like jewels, the work of the hands of a cunning workman.

"Thy navel is like a round goblet, which wanteth not liquor; thy belly is like an heap of wheat set about with lilies.

"Thy two breasts are like two young roes that are twins."

There are various readings in the Bible dealing with sodomy, incest, and multiple sex partners;[14] and, the romantic verses in The Song of Solomon, previously referred to, actually continue for several chapters.[15]

Certainly we are all interested in sex and sex-related matters. This great drive, ostensibly designed by the Creator,[16] interested the writers of the Bible and its present-day advocates as well, no matter how much they feign personal disinterest.

Preachers and Sex

For some reason preachers don't like to talk about sex except in depreciative terms. Somewhere along the line the church got the notion that sex was not for recreation but solely for procreation; and the least said about the whole thing, the better.

Some priests are not permitted by their church to marry and have sought sexual gratification elsewhere, occasionally running afoul of the law in these attempts. There is a reliable report that one lawyer alone has handled over 225 law suits against priests accused of molesting children.[17] Other priests have established various types of covert liaisons or formally withdrawn from the priesthood to find a wife or other sexual companion. Strange how millions of people — men and women — get their sexual guidance from a cleric who claims infallibility, wears a dress, and has never been married.

So the preacher you see in the pulpit Sunday morning, resplendent in his priestly robes, will either avoid the subject of sex or inveigh against it, except within the marital contract. His wife, however, sitting primly in her pew, probably gussied to the gills, will know the diverse proclivities of the disrobed preacher — may even wish he would be more interested in sex, this man we call "the reverend." Why these people seek to deny sexual relief and release to the unmarried is a mystery.

Sex Is Sin Number One
As a result largely of church pressure, high sin has come to be synonymous with non-marital sex; and, for some churches, sex

should not be recreational even within the marital contract. Capital punishment and war are all necessary concomitants of life to them, but non-procreational sex is anathema for these people — or so they say.

Yes, at least by proclamation, sex for fun is sin number one. As an example of social over-reaction to unconventional sexual activity, there was a widely circulated account of a school teacher who had been charged with having sex with some of her pupils. Her bail was set at $1 million. Unable to raise sufficient bond money, she was sent to the county jail to await trial.[18] On the same day, in the same county, a man was arrested for attempted murder and for using a firearm in the commission of a felony. His bail was set at $13 thousand. He made bail and was released pending trial.[19] These two cases, juxtaposed, show the unusual weight our society places on unconventional sexual activities. How foolish!

Is there one among us who does not have in the back of his or her mind some past sexual experience that we either value or despise, depending on our perspective and the circumstances surrounding the incident? Did we play "doctor" as a child? Has what was enjoyed at the time, become poisoned by professional counsellors who feel a need to be on the "good" side of a highly emotional issue to insure their professional status with the public, their colleagues and the church?

Drumming Up Sin

In Napa, California, there is an activist group called the "False Memory Syndrome Foundation" which works in behalf of people who say they have been unjustly accused of sexual abuse.[20] Often in such cases the accuser has been under the guidance of one or more "therapists" who use what has been called "recovery-memory" therapy which tries to unlock memories of childhood traumas.

There are other such groups in our country that seek to protect people from false-accusers, who may be their own grown children, that have encountered some problem in their lives, and sought help from a professional counselor or social worker. Often attempts to unlock repressed memories are conducted by using sodium pentothal or some other barbiturate so that the interviews are conducted with the patient in a highly relaxed atmosphere with the patient readily receptive to the suggestions of the therapist.

A case has been reported in which as many as 141 injections of sodium pentathol were administered over a relatively short period of time, leaving the patient in a near vegetable condition.[21] This case indicates the lengths some so-called therapists will go to elicit desired information. Guided imagery, and graphic visualizations have sometimes led to the creation of false memories. In layman's terms, these memory seekers use a form of hypnosis, and out of their suggestive therapy can come an erroneous conviction on the part of the patient that he or she was sexually abused during childhood.

Startled parents of grown children are occasionally confronted with an accusation that they molested one or more of their children years earlier, the accusation being totally false and — of all things — suggested by a professional "therapist." In one such case a woman was seeking help for being overweight. Here the therapist concluded the patient had been sexually abused as a child by her father. The patient, now a grown woman, confronted her father who was nonplused. It was later shown conclusively that such abuse never occurred.[22]

Both supporters and opponents of repressed memory therapy or, as it has been called, "hypno-therapy," and other forms of memory inducement, welcome the intense study now being given this field by the American Psychological Association. Such studies were begun after prominent people in the field of medicine expressed concerns about such forms of memory inducement. One such personage was Dr. Judith L. Herman, professor of psychiatry at the Harvard medical school.[23]

The possibilities for abuse by a specialist with a strong anti-sex bias is evident. A social worker with a fundamentalist, anti-sex orientation, would also be a candidate for imparting such manufactured memory; and, all people who deal with children are, to some degree, at risk.

Sexual Orientation

One's sexual orientation is formed by many factors including heredity. What a person is in most any aspect of his or her life is a product of birth and experience.[24] If a certain group mounted a campaign against people with blue eyes — let us say that one of their prophets had said or written that blue eyes are a sign of demonic character — then perfectly innocent blue-eyed people would be shunned by that group. So it has been with homosexuals and other sexual non-conformists.

Homosexuality is a minority sexual orientation castigated in the Bible by the apostle Paul and other biblical writers;[25] s o there are many fired-up by the Bible and their own self-righteousness, and a possible lack of sexual adjustment, who vigorously oppose this minority group. Again, we find the fundamentalist evangelicals on their crusading horses riding off in all directions trying to tell others how to conduct their lives.

Well, then, what about homosexuality, is it a sin? Of course not. It is perfectly natural. Animals mount each other, including those of the same sex. Cattle breeders have a name for this: they call it "bulling." We all have some of this sexual drive. In the avowed homosexual, the urge is more powerful than in the heterosexual. It is this latent feeling of homosexuality that so disturbes the homophobic and makes him feel the need to prove his "straightness" — both to himself, and to others — by getting on the record as opposed to homosexuality.

Then what about masturbation? Is it natural? Do animals masturbate? You bet. Ask any cattleman if bulls do not relieve their sexual needs, on occasions, simulating the sex act by moving their penis in its sheath until they ejaculate. Cows mount each other in simulation of intercourse.

And what about oral sex? In the old law this was referred to as a "crime against nature." Truth is, as everyone knows, animals are regularly sniffing and licking the genitalia of their own kind. So oral sex is far from being unnatural.

Thus what happens among consenting parties; i.e., the way in which they please each other sexually, is their own concern and not that of the religious right. The old, the unattractive, the handicapped, and those who just plain want a non-marital sexual experience, but are unable to attract a suitable sexual partner, should not be intimidated by those that claim to be in touch with God who has directed them to "save" unmarried people seeking responsible sexual satisfaction.

But no matter who you are, remember: Those fundamentalists want to get inside your head and expunge those "dirty thoughts"!

The subject of sex should be brought from the sleaze parlor into the arena of rational discussion. Sex and fantasy go hand-in-hand. What "turns you on" is highly subjective. Yet the radical religionist would have you believe that you are in for eternal damnation unless you have only conventional sex and have it within a marital context — preferably in a marriage performed within a church, or at least under religious aegis.

They hold that sex is sin if it deviates from the traditional mount-and-ride, never-mention-it-again type of experience within the bonds of matrimony. But each of us — including the fundamentalists — have handled our sexual parts with pleasure and fantasized about a wide range of activities assisted, at times, by some form of "marital" or visual aid, and/or our imagination. It may be that it is in this area that the strong sex drive of the teenager can be released with a resulting sharp drop in unwanted pregnancies. Still you had better watch those dirty thoughts, according to the fundamentalist, or God will get you!

Protecting Our Sexual Freedoms

In reality, what a wonderful experience sex can be. We are all here as a result of sex, and it is doubtful if the most pious married couple has sex only for procreation. Thus, as distinguised from crimes of passion, such as rape or assault of various types, most everyone has had or is having sex. Nothing is more normal. Why let the church tell us what kind of sex to have? We should be free to enjoy our lives and its necessary and desirable functions without officious intermeddling so long as we are not coercing others or otherwise forcing them to do what they do not wish to do.

How many women have had their lives destroyed by the self-righteous, for having a child out of wedlock? Happily such social opprobrium is waning and responsible single parenting is increasingly acceptable. This is proving to be a God-send to many women who simply cannot find, for various reasons, a suitable husband, and who have the financial ability to raise a child alone.

Despite this more reasoned social view, there are many still among us determined to tell us how to conduct our sex life. It is absolutely nobody's business what you read or otherwise view; yet, there are the fundamentalist busy bodies that enjoy the self-righteous feeling they get by joining some church group that wants to-go-a-banning this or that library book or video store's sexually explicit materials. Often they comb store shelves and come up with lists of material we are not supposed to read. Often these lists are not confined to sexual materials.

Such lists are often broadened to include material they refer to as "satanic" or "cultist." The *Three Little Pigs* and *Little Red Riding Hood* have appeared on some lists of books to be banned at the local school library. At a high school in Florida, students involved in editing the school newspaper were told by a school official to delete the word "earlobes" from an article they were about to print. It was done. Too risque to print, was the reported cause of this censorship. In any case, it was the epitome of buffoonery. Even the extreme left gets into the act by opposing *Little Black Sambo,* and the American classics, *Tom Sawyer* and *Huckleberrry Finn,* and the stories of *Uncle Remus* and *Brer Rabbit*; so watch out for those revisionists as well as those far-out fundamentalists![26]

Responsible Sex

No reasonable person argues for irresponsible sex or sex where force or coercion is used. A person's private parts should be untouched by others unless consent is freely given. What is objected to here are those who mount campaigns to keep others from enjoying consensual sex. Such efforts are usually carried on by those who are married and presumably having sex. It may be that they are unable to enjoy the sex they have due to ingrained anti-sex indoctrination by the church, and substitute the good feeling of self-righteousness for the good feeling of a good sexual relationship.

Local state's attorneys are often badgered by fundamentalist "family" groups into conducting raids on mom and pop book and video stores. It may be that those who join these religious consorship groups seek to expunge their own guilt feelings, at having recreational sex, by keeping others from its joys. Certainly the energy spent in such censorship raids could be better spent being concerned with raising teacher salaries, and otherwise supporting education and other worthy causes.

Sexual harassment is sexual assault, with or without touching. The difficulty here lies in the fact that so many — men in particular — do not know how to relate to those of the opposite sex. In their sexual and social awkwardness, they may be guilty of acting in a crude, vulgar, and otherwise embarrassing and distasteful way. The recipient of such comments, gesturing, or touching should unhesitatingly rebuff such individuals in no uncertain terms and protest to a higher level of authority, should the harassment persist and their protestations not honored.

Notes

1. WFA Women's Commission, collation number 2, 2361 Friendship Road, Waldoboro, Maine, August, 1994, p.23.

2. Supra.

3. Supra.

4. Supra.

5. Supra.

6. Supra, p. 25.

7. Supra.

8. Genesis 24:16,43; Exodus 22:17; Leviticus 21:3, 13,14; Deuteronomy 17:20; 22:15,19,23,28; 32:25; Judges 11:37,38; 21:12; Second Samuel 13:2,18; First Kings 1:2; Second Kings 19:21; Esther 2:2,3,17,19; Psalms 45:14; Isaiah 7:14; 23:4,12; 37:22; 47:1; 62:5; Jeremiah 14:17; 18:13; 31:4,13,21; 46:11; Lamentations 1:4,15,18; 2:10,13,21; Joel 1:8; Amos 5:2; 8:13; Ezekiel 23:3,8; The Song of Solomon 1:3; 6:8; Matthew 1:23; 25:1,7,11; Luke 1:27; 2:36; Acts 21:9; First Corinthians 7:25,28,34,37: Second Corinthians 11:2; Revelation 14:4.

9. Genesis 17:11-27.

10. Genesis 17:10.

11. Genesis 17:15-17; 9:29 (Noah 950 years); Genesis 5:3-4 (Adam 930 years); Genesis 5:6-7 (Seth 912 years); Genesis 5:9-10 (Enos 905 years); Genesis 5:18-20 (Jared 962 years); Genesis 5:25-27 (Methuselah 969 years).

12. Genesis 5:6-7; 25-27.

13. Genesis 17:15-17.

14. The Song of Solomon 7:1-3; Other examples of explicit sex: Genesis 16:1-6 (adultery); Genesis 19:1-8 (sodomy); Genesis 19:30-38 (repeated incest). For references to multiple sex partners (concubinage), see: Daniel 5; Judges 8,19,20; Second Samuel 3,5,15,16,19-21; First Kings 11; First Chronicles 1,2,37; Second Chronicles 11; Esther 2; The Song of Solomon 6.

15. The Song of Solomon; chapters 1-8.

16. Colossians 1:16; John 1:3; Epheisans 3:9; Psalms 33:6.

17. Milo Geyelin, *The Catholic Church Struggles With Suits Over Sexual Abuse,* Wall Street Journal, November 24, 1993.

18. See: Florida Today, Melbourne, Florida, August 25, 1994.

19. Supra.

20. Milo Geyelin, *Lawsuits Over False Memories Face Hurdles*, Wall Street Journal, May 17, 1994. See: Dorothy Rabinowitz, *A Darkness in Massachusetts II*, Wall Street Journal, March 14, 1995.

21. Supra.

22. Supra.

23. Supra.

24. *Brain Study Suggests Biology Plays Role In Sexual Orientation,* Associated Press release in Florida Today, Melbourne, Florida; November 18, 1994.

25. Romans 1:24-32. See also: Leviticus 18:22, et al.

26. See: Florida Today, Melbourne, Florida, February 15, 1995, p. 10A. Also see: Brumsic Brandon, *Revisionists Cause Brer Rabbit Hard Times,* Florida Today, Melbourne, Florida, March 18, 1995.

CREATION AND RELIGION

The Falacy of Free Moral Agency

From an ethical and religious point of view it appears that the creative force that set all reproductive forces in being left to random chance the length, type and quality of our lives. The notion that we are watched over by a loving, all-powerful, protector and that our problems are of our own doing, hardly conforms to today's scientific and experential evidence.

Nowhere is this more strikingly evident than in the study of genetically transmitted diseases and abnormalities. Many illnesses and bodily disfunctions are not the punishment for "sinning," but rather the result of a diabolically conceived reproduction system wherein even children can suffer horribly, and die at an early age, because of their genetic makeup over which they had and have no control.

Even if we were to eventually find cures for all genetic abnormalities, those people who, in the past, have suffered so greatly, are mute evidence of the diabolical nature of the reproductive system.

Churches usually take no notice of these facts.

Many disabling and fatal diseases have proven to be gene-oriented. In large measure the chance of a person leading a normal life is due to the luck-of-the-draw at conception. A person may get, for example, the gene that gives one a disposition to have breast or colon cancer, or any of a wide variety of disastrous illnesses. Thus the relating of a person's "sin" or malefaction to his or her health may often prove incorrect.

It may well be that a person's sickness or disability has nothing to do with his actions, but rather is caused by genetic makeup over which he or she had no control. It is perfectly logical to expect some products of such a diabolical system to act diabolically; and we should not be surprised if some of these individuals rebel at their unjust fate.

The idea that we are "free moral agents" — a favorite term of the religious fundamentalists — and that we can make of ourselves what we will, or that there is some benevolent higher power that watches over us, protecting us, is experientially and scientifically not true. Again, the idea promoted by the religious right that we are watched over by a higher power that dispenses even-handed justice to his believers is patently untrue. Let us look at some of the evidence.

Each of us is the product of thousands of genes passed to us by our ancestors.[1] We are just beginning to understand the profound effect these genes, sewn into the reproductive process at creation, have on our individual make-ups. Happily, biotechnology offers some hope for those who suffer from such genetic weaknesses.

For example, Dr. Cesare Sirtori has apparently found a family with an inherited genetic abnomality that limits the build-up of fatty deposits which can cause heart attacks and strokes. His discovery might lead to the finding of a genetic material that can allow patients with high levels of cholesterol to produce their own plaque control with their own bodies.[2]

Heart attacks leave useless scar tissue. By regulating the body's genes, it is thought this scar tissue might be turned into muscle tissue. This work is proceeding at Southwestern Medical Center in Dallas and at the University of Southern California.[3]

Some six years ago a gene called Myo D was found to be able to turn almost any cell in the body into a muscle cell. Working with animals, Dr. Laurence Kedes of USC found some heart scar tissue could be turned into muscle tissue by the use of Myo D. At this time it is unclear if this muscle tissue can conduct electricity and beat like the muscle it is intended to replace.[4] But there is hope here.

One out of five people are affected in some degree with the learning disorder called dyslexia which refers to an inordinate difficulty in processing words and sounds. This disfunction causes enormous emotional and social damage. Experts now feel dyslexia is genetically transmitted.[5]

A neuropsychologist and research director at the National Institute of Child Health and Human development has said that dyslexia generally remains with a person all his or her life causing continual learning problems for its victims.[6]

A federal advisory panel has recommended research using human embryos in order to provide valuable insights into the causes of infertility, genetic diseases, and cancer. The panel said the use of human embryos in research "warrants serious moral consideration." It continued, an embryo is "a developing form of human life, and doesn't have the same moral status as infants and children."[7]

One source of embryos could be private invitro fertilization clinics which sometimes have embryos which, for various reasons, were not implanted in a woman's uterus.

John Fletcher, director of the Center for Biomedical Ethics at the University of Virginia, notes that some child cancers begin in the embryo. "To avoid answering the question of how these disorders begin is a terrible disservice to living children with cancer," he observed.[8]

Scientists now know that some people have "diseased genes" as part of their DNA. For example, gene BRCA1 and BRCA2 are inherited and can cause breast cancer. It is believed 85% of women with the breast cancer gene will develop breast cancer.[9]

Will families in the future with cancer genes, or other dreaded disease genes in their DNA, choose not to reproduce or abort fetuses, or not marry for fear of passing along some deadly gene they may carry? Will DNA profiles eventually be used in the selection of a spouse?

From a religious standpoint, what justifies this pre-punishment? That is, why does a just creator pre-doom certain individuals to one or more terrible diseases before they have even been born? The idea of a good life for the "good" and damnation for the "sinner" looks more specious the more scientific evidence we uncover. In fact, this evidence increasingly points to a horrendous — or at best an amoral — creative force that dooms people before they have had a chance to interact with their environment.

It would seem that disease genes which are likely to kill a person in childhood would soon disappear from the human gene pool because the victim has little chance of passing them on. But here the diabolical nature of reproduction is reinforced as researchers have uncovered evidence that some genetic diseases are produced only when a person inherits a "bad" gene from each parent.

This is the case with sickle-cell anemia. The gene remains in the population because most carriers have only one copy of the gene. Apparently cystic fibrosis is the same sort of gene in the sense that one afflicted with the disease has received a mutated version of the gene CFTR from both parents.[10]

Research at the John Radcliffe Hospital in Oxford, England, has found that children with malaria who also have a gene called TNF2 are seven times as likely to have their malaria result in a fatal brain disorder.[11] There are other such gene-transmitted diseases. One of these is Tay-Sachs disease, a fatal metabolic disorder. that can result if the gene is inherited in duplicate.[12]

The reverse side of this "bad" gene story is the fact that some of these so-called "bad" genes have the ability to do "good": A single TNF2 gene can enhance the immune system and give carriers of the single gene a survival advantage over those who do not carry the gene.[13]

Some genes that can kill if received from both parents, may actually be life-enhancing if received from only one parent. Another such gene is CFTR. While it can cause cystic fibrosis if received from both parents, a single such gene can provide protection against cholera.[14]

Some people are thus doomed by their DNA; others with no major DNA problems, can live normal lives. It is a matter of pure chance. A part of the very structure and design of creation.

Addendum

Laura was but five years old, yet she died two months after her second multiple organ transplant having received seven organs: liver, stomach, pancreas, large and small intestines, and two kidneys to correct short-gut syndrome, an intestinal deformity.

She also had cancer-like growths that were started by the Epstein-Barr virus.

Some people criticized her parents for putting their daughter through so much pain and suffering.

Her doctor said it would have been unfair to the child not to try every possible method of treatment since she had never known any "meaningful survival."

During her final days she wished to be an angel in the Christmas play. Laura died before she could realize her wish.[15]

How can we reconcile this true story with church teachings that there is a just, good, and all-powerful Creator?[16]

In varying degrees the fate of Laura is that of millions of children and adults who suffer and die never really having known "meaningful survival."

If there is a lesson in Laura's story, it is that the society should pursue every lead to help such people who have been so unfairly treated by the very essence of creation. Such a search for the relief of these suffering people clearly includes embryo, and other forms of genetic research. We must not be deterred in this search by religious fanatics.

Notes

1. George Melloan, *The "Bell Curve" Sells Genetic Science Short*, Wall Street Journal, October 31, 1994.

2. Supra.

3. *Researchers Probe Muscle Gene Therapy*, Associated Press, Florida Today, Melbourne, Florida, November 16, 1994.

4. Supra.

5. *Experts Suspect Gene As Cause For Dyslexia*, Newsday. See: Florida Today, Melbourne, Florida, October 14, 1994.

6. Supra.

7. Laurie McGinley, *Research That Uses Human Embryos Should Get U.S. Funding, Panel Says*. Wall Street Journal, September 28, 1994.

8. Supra.

9. Ellen Goodman, syndicated columnist, *Breast Cancer Gene Brings New Questions*. See: Florida Today, Melbourne, Florida, September 20, 1994.

10. Rick Weiss of the Washington Post, *Bad Genes May Be The Good Ones To Have..* See: Florida Today, Melbourne, Florida, October 16, 1994.

11. Supra.

12. Supra.

13. Supra.

14. Supra.

15. Jeffrey Bair, Associated Press, *Laura's Dreams Of Being Play's Angel Die With Her.*

69

See: Florida Today, Melbourne, Florida, November 12, 1993.

16. God is just: Deuteronomy 32:4; Isaiah 45:21; see: Job 4:17; 9:2; 33:12; 34:17; Psalms 7:9; Zephaniah 3:5; Acts 3:14; 22:14; Romans 3:21-26. God is good: Matthew 19:17; Mark 10:18; Luke 18:19. God is all-powerful: Matthew 19:26; Mark 10:27; 14:36; Luke 18:27; compare: Mark 9:23. God is creator of all things in heaven and earth: Colossians 1:16; compare: John 1:3; Ephesians 3:9; Psalms 33:6.

CRIME, PUNISHMENT, AND THE BIBLE

Individual Criminal Liability for National Leaders

Individual leadership liability is essential to a world system of justice. For example, ethnic cleansing, civilian bombardment, and many other violations of human rights, set in motion by national leaders, are crimes against humanity. They violate universal laws of human behavior established by the Nurenberg and Tokyo war crimes trials, by the United Nations charter and other documents[1.] Those who perpetrate these crimes must be held accountable to a world court that reflects humanity's outrage.

At present we tend to use military intervention or economic blockades and boycotts to correct human rights violations at the national and multi-national levels. Often these efforts go on for years and fall heaviest on the innocent poor who cannot afford the blackmarket prices it takes to lead a normal life under such circumstances. On the other hand, those guilty of crimes against humanity are in a postion to afford the amenities of life, including retirement with a substantial pension.

Therefore, the very best deterrent is to hold such malefactors personally liable for their human rights violations. By so doing, those who are in a position to commit war crimes, or other major human rights violations, would stand to lose not only their international mobility and personal freedoms, but their wealth as well.

Although it may be impractical to effect the immediate apprehension of such national leaders, they should be made to know, well in advance, that there will be no permanent hiding place should they violate human rights. Their actions against their own and other people will be documented for later trial by a tribunal representing humanity's outrage. There can simply be no effective deterrent to human rights violations at the national and multi-national levels if leaders are alowed to brutalize people under the guise of quelling civil disturbances, annexing territories, protecting ethnic or religious practices, or some other pretext.

Great powers with the ability to invade foreign countries and capture errant foreign leaaders will have difficulties acting unilaterally. There is an inherent resentment of power, even among victims of power abuse. Military intervention can galvanize internal opposition and swing the populace of the country invaded into a "protect the motherland" frenzy which can play right into the hands of the human rights violating leadership. Apprehension of a human rights violator under these conditions may be not only difficult, but nearly impossible without doing more harm than good and getting bogged down militarily in such a unilateral arrest attempt.

More effective would be a multi-national force, preferably under United Nations auspicies. Also needed would be a prior world consensus focused on each particular criminal and his illegal activities. The United Nations is clearly best suited for such a task. Even the UN will find such operations difficult, even if occasionally necessary.

Modern nations no longer mull or linger over what constitutes "human rights."[2] The spadework in this area has been done for years through the efforts of many, including Thomas Jefferson, who wrote that the Founding Fathers found these truths to be self-evident: "that all men are created equal, that they are endowed by their Creator with certain unalienable Rights, that among these are Life, Liberty and the pursuit of Happiness. — That to secure these rights, Governments are institued among Men. . . ."[3]

Registry of Crimes and Criminals

Again, the names and the misdeeds of those who violate human rights must be entered into an international criminal record for the purpose of later bringing such individuals to trial and punishment. In the future, responsiblity must go hand-in-hand with authority. To be a world or national leader will be to make one's actions liable to an accounting and subject to the scrutiny of world opinion. A person who uses his political power to violate human rights and world consensus will be designated a world outlaw and be subject to being brought to the bar of international justice. No longer will thousands die in response to the orders of criminal national and world leaders only to have those leaders remain in power or retreat to some safe haven to live out their lives in security and luxury. Responsibility will, in the future, be part and parcel of national and international leadership.

Humanitarian Relief

What sometimes begins as humanitarian relief from one nation to another, often developes a military component with human suffering exacerbated rather than relieved. Only in extreme cases should international armed force be introduced into a nation's internal problems, and then only when there are clearly defined goals to be sought with limited time parameters, and United Nations approval.

Nation-building should be left to individual nations as a rule. But when their leaders violate human rights, they must be declared international criminals subject to arrest and trial when they journey outside their own nation. Sometimes this will require both vigilance and patience on behalf of the outside world.

Such opprobrium for and action against national and international criminal leaders will be a powerful lever to protect the innocent from human rights abuses by zealous leaders bent on carrying out their intra-national and international designs.

The Treatment of Prisoners Generally

One of our great social mistakes is the way we treat our prisoners, both domestic and international. When a crime is commited, shall we commit a second crime, in effect, by killing or simply warehousing the perpetrator? Generally what has happened is that some individual, family, or group has been wronged as in rape, robbery, or any of a vast number of other human rights violations.

A "debt," if you will, has thereby been created by the wrongdoer to a specific individual, and/or a group of individuals and to the society generally, as in war crimes and other large scale, mass human rights violations. How is this debt repaid by warehousing or taking the life of the criminal?

It costs the equivalent of a year's tuition at Harvard to keep a person in jail for one year. To keep a juvenile in reform school for one year costs $50,000.[4] The argument is made that incarceration is a deterrent and that the criminal is paying back his "debt to society" simply through the loss of his freedom. The public's attitude is often to "put him away and throw away the key" without reckoning the costs to the taxpayer and others. Little or no thought is given to the billions of dollars it costs to house and care for criminals generally, long after the wrong has become a statistic and society has forgotten the offense. Taxpayers are, in effect, awarding long-time scholarships for the advanced study of crime, as the system now stands.

One visit to a prison can be enough to keep many from risking loss of freedom through the commission of a crime. Certainly school children in the higher grades should have the chance to tour a nearby prison as a part of their social studies.

The vast majority of people sent to prison are held too long. Prison becomes a school for crime after the person jailed has lost all hope and self-respect. Again, prisons are schools for crime bought and paid for by taxpayers. Generally speaking, long-time warehousing should be limited to repeat offenders. So many people, including drug offenders, are sent to prison simply to sit in cages with nothing to do and without help in the reconstruction of their lives.

Compensation for Victims of Crime

Much better, and clearly more economical than simply warehousing criminals, would be to lessen the length of sentences and use the money saved to train those in jail, looking to the day of their constructive return to society. Remember, most prisoners do not return to prison. Shall they be trained in a trade other than crime? Absolutely. Anger and retribution do not heal the damage done by the commission of a crime. Those injured by crime should be compensated as nearly as possible for their loss by the criminal who has harmed them.

It was once thought impossible to repay an injury. The question was asked: How much should one be paid for hurting? or, put another way, what is the money value of, say, the loss of an eye or limb? Now through workman's compensation legislation and insurance formulations we have set monetary values for personal, emotional and physical injuries as well as for property damages. Thus, there is now ample basis for determining within reasonable parameters just how much a criminal should pay his victim for pain, suffering, and property loss.

Some of this compensation can be made through work done in prison; and there can be the constructive coupling of such prison training and work done during post release employment. Does this make the prisons "debtor prisons," and training schools? To some extent they should be training schools, but the term "debtor's prison" has historically meant a prison for those failing to pay a civil, not a criminal, debt. We are dealing here with obligations incurred as a result of crime.

Since prisons are now post graduate schools for the advanced study of crime, and victims of crimes are not assisted in their rehabilitative recovery by having their violator imprisoned for years; our attention should shift from a retribution mode to one of compensation for the victims of crime. And although he may get a perverse satisfaction out of knowing his violator is "wasting away" in jail; the victim and society are poorly served by such a condition.

What to Do

Several things can be done: We can begin to change the law violator so he will not be a recidivist. This means we must first apprehend the perpetrator of crime be he local petty criminal or an international leader who has committed a war crime or other violation of human rights.

After apprehension there must be treatment — not just loss of freedom — for the criminal. In most cases such treatment can be effected in a short period of time. It is the early part of incarceration that offers the greatest hope; that period before total despair and loss of incentive sets in. It is the time frame within which attitudes can be changed and new motivations instilled; it can be too late after a prolonged, personality deadening stretch of time, which so many now undergo.

Also we should address the "debt" owed the victim by the criminal. It may take a lifetime to repay. Whatever period of time is involved, this period would be an investment for society, the victim, and the criminal, as opposed to the time now wasted sitting in jail at great cost to taxpayers and with nothing being done for the victims of crime.

Under the proposed program, the criminal is constantly reminded by his pay-backs that he has committted a wrong and that the price of that wrong is very high. At the same time the victim is not allowed to twist in the wind, but gets regular compensation from the one who has injured him.

This compensation of the victim, provided by the criminal, can be earned both in and, later, out of jail. Judges and the law can establish the amount of these payments which will vary according to the severity of the crime involved and the circumstances surrounding the criminal; e.g., his age, abilities and training. But the criminal is to be kept working and paying to his victim. This process makes the criminal a productive, learning, motivated, and taxpaying individual, as opposed to — in effect — a dangerous, caged animal in training to be more vicious.

Remember the vast majority of prisoners will be released after some period of time, even under the present system. It is to everyone's advantage that this released offender behave in a socially responsible way. It should be emphasized that such a program of incarceration, training, work, release, and payback, will apply to every type of criminal, except the incorrigible. Included should be international leaders guilty of crimes against humanity. Except the international human rights violator's paybacks will go to assist, as nearly as possible, those groups whose human rights he is responsible for violating. Regional world courts, with the right of appeal to a supreme world court, must be set in place.

There is often the understandable emotional reaction by the victims of crime and their families. They may want to have the criminal "punished to the full extent of the law." In some cases, in those states that have capital punishment, this can mean death. What is missing from such visceral responses to crime is that there is no correction of the criminal, or damages to be repaid, in the reasoning of the victim. His desire, at the time of sentencing, is simply to have the perverse satisfaction of knowing the one who has harmed him will be "wasting away" in jail.

At this point in the sentencing process a presiding judge must not be swayed by these emotions of revenge and hatred on the part of the victim(s) of crime; the judge must not lose sight of the long-term opportunity for correction and compensation that are involved. So often the public says, in effect, it does not believe in redemption or change on the part of the criminal; yet, a human's ability to change is a tenet at the very heart of Christianity. Once a criminal, always a criminal is the fundamemtalist attitude, thus branding an offender for life. Again, it is the obligation of the presiding judge at sentencing, to set the tone for constructive rehabilitation and "debt" repayment by the criminal.

But the courts are not insensitive to the political ramifications of sentencing. A judge may well be inclined to listen to the public clamor and to impose a long jail term by sending the offender away to vegetate at length at taxpayer's expense without provision for training or payback. This is a reflex action bottomed on the notion that punishment only is the judge's task. But this does not compensate the victim of the crime, nor does it diminish the likelihood of a repeat offense — all hallmarks of constructive sentencing by a good jurist.

Some criminals, sentenced to long terms behind bars, may become anesthetized by their stay in jail and return to society embittered and bent on "getting even" with the system that put them away. Jails should be correctional institutions in more than name. But all too frequently they are graduate schools for advancing criminal careers. For the sake of the victims of crime and for taxpayers generally, the penal system must change.

Capital Punishment

By eliminating the barbaric practice of capital punishment, the savings to the taxpayers would be considerable. The average prison inmate on death row remains there an average of just under 10 years waiting to die, while appeals are taken and other legal machinery is employed. The taxpayer's costs per death row inmate is over $3 million.

The answer to this problem for all involved is not to lessen the legal rights of those convicted of capital crimes; but, rather, to abolish capital punishment. This uncivilized and un-Christian practice is the epitome of cruel and unusual punishment that should have no place in our society. Ironically, the costs of capital punishment are greater than the $700 thousand it costs to keep a prisoner in jail for life. It is not only far less than the cost of capital punishment, it serves to illustrate the monumental costs of both capital punishment and extended imprisonments.

While there may be those who may need to be institutionalized for life, in the vast majority of cases, it would be far better for taxpayers and the victims of crime, to employ training and early release. Simply warehousing those convicted of crime for extended periods of time produces additonal hatred of society and repeat offenders, rather than taxpaying, constructive future citizens who can leave prison, uplift the society, and pay to their victims and the taxpaying public at least some of the costs involved in their crime, trial, and subsequent imprisonment.

Capital punishment is apparently supported by the vast majority of so-called Christians. Ironically the cross, symbol of the horrors of capital punishment, is prominently displayed in and on practically every Christian church in the world. Yet while the judgment against Christ is recognized today as wrong, the fundamentalist church leadership roundly applauds capital punishment.

There is the additional element of "cruel and unusual punishment," as one under a death sentence awaits his fate behind bars constantly seeking and hoping for a reprieve or judical reversal, or at least a stay of execution.

In most cases, and at the time of trial and sentencing, a judgment could be entered in favor of the victim in an appropriate amount. Such award would be recorded in a central data bank available to anyone who may wish to employ the defendant after an award has been rendered against him and he is released from prison; the debt to be stricken from the record when it has been paid in full.

Again, this means that one who criminally injures another is to pay for that injury much as one who is civilly wronged, as in a traffic or other personal injury case.

Thus one convicted of a crime and placed on probation or parol, would have a portion of all he earns paid to the clerk of court where the crime occurred, for the benefit of the victim or his family. Monies earned inside prison would also be used to help the victims of crime.

Such a system would cause the public and the victims of crimes to be more agreeable to earlier releases from prison because the sooner out of jail the quicker the wrongdoer can be able to find a better paying job than his prison job and thereby be able to make larger payments on his debt to the victim and his family. But we must remember that in today's technologically oriented world, job training is a necessity for most meaningful employment.

The criminal should be given every opportunity in jail to train himself for a useful, skilled job and early release. This would be a powerful incentive to behave in prison, reducing prison disturbances and the costs of prison security, maintenance and operation.

So many prisoners — one immediately thinks of evangelists serving prison terms for fraud — are good bets, under minimum surveillance, to be harmless and constructive outside prison. There is absolutely no need to keep some people in jail years on end — no need to rob them of all dignity and self-respect so they become hardened and so anti-social they return to society more criminally bent than when they entered prison. Our prisons should not be institutions for criminal learning, but centers of rehabilitation.

Creative Sentencing

Creative sentencing involves the lessening — and in some cases, the elimination — of jail time. Sentencing experts are to become involved at the judge's request. This will involve parole officers, doctors, lawyers, people in municipal government, and whomever the court feels might be of assistance. Their task will be to put together sentencing ideas appropriate to the criminal and his crime with a view toward rehabilitating the offender and compensating his victim and society.

Present tight budgets and overcrowded jails should speed the day when government takes a new, and hopefully uplifting, look at the present penal system and makes it more responsive and helpful to the needs of the victims of crime, taxpayers, and those among us who commit crimes. Fixed jail terms, more prisons, and the elimination of parole, are not long-term solutions to our crime problem, either from an economic or humanitarian standpoint.

People convicted of small but jailable offenses can be kept out of jail by the use of creative sentencing. One judge, in addition to suspended sentencing, required young offenders to successfully complete their high school training or its equivalent (GED). In their "off" time these offenders were to do public works in order to compensate their victims.

Another such alternative sentence involved a youngster convicted of putting graffiti on a public wall. He was sentenced to guard the wall during certain hours for a six month period and to remove his own and other graffiti.[5]

Community service, such as cleaning parks, buildings, and roadways has resulted in large savings to the taxpayers in certain areas where it has been conscientiously tried.[6]

There has been developed what are called "special service crews." In one area of California some 10,000 people served out their sentences by painting over graffiti, cleaning-up trash, pulling weeds, and doing maintenance work for their communities. Crews were monitored so the prescribed hours of community service were actually performed. It is estimated the taxpayers of the area were saved the sum of $80 million by this program over a 10 year period. [7]

Corporal Punishment

Flogging, the rack, hot-poker, and pressing were in the minds of the Founding Fathers who remembered the fate of those found guilty of religious unorthodoxy by the Inquisition in Europe, and by various courts in this country.[8] Today corporal punishment has been left to another age, except we still practice capital punishment and beat our children in the public schools.

Yes, we do not whip our criminals anymore, but we do whip our children and — of all places — in the public schools!

Humanitarian punishment is not a matter of country, and its standards should apply universally. When an American teenager living in Singapore was sentenced to be beaten with a cane for spray-painting graffiti, the case became a cause célèbre.[9] Even the president of the United States sought to prevent the "caning." One interesting aspect of this case was that there was no ground-swell of protest led by our nation's churches.

Why do we continue to allow the whipping of our children in the public schools? The answer probably lies in the thought that if we "spare the rod,"we will "spoil the child." This nonsense finds its roots in such biblical passages as: "Withhold not correction from the child: for if thou beatest (sic) him with the rod, he shall not die. Thou shall beat him with the rod, and shall deliver his soul from hell."[10]

There are other such sickening admonitions in the Bible to use the "rod": "And if a man smite his servant, or his maid (sic), with a rod, and he die under his hand; he shall be surely punished. Notwithstanding, if he continue a day or two, he shall not be punished: for he is his money."[11] Apparently you can beat your servant half to death, just be sure you don't kill him or her!

There is another such admonition to use beatings: "In the lips of him that hath understanding wisdom is found: but a rod is for the back of him that is void of understanding."[12] Here, evidently, the slow learner may be beaten with impunity.

Now listen to this: "He that spareth his rod hateth his son: but he that loveth him chasteneth him betimes."[13] Yes, beat the boy only occasionally! It's enough to make one wonder, if he didn't know better, if the fundamentalists ever read what's in the Bible they claim to take literally. More biblical advice on corporal punishment: "foolishness is bound in the heart of a child; but the rod of correction shall drive it far from him"[14] and, "If his children forsake my law, and walk not in my judgments; if they break my statutes, and keep not my commandments, then shall I visit their transgression with the rod, and their iniquity with stripes;" and, "Chasten thy son while there is hope, and let not thy soul spare for his crying."[15] Yes, evidently we should keep flogging those children. Ridiculous!

So you see the genesis of the phrase "spare the rod and spoil the child," lies in the Bible. This official sanction "from God," as it were, is used to justify — even compel — the whipping of children and others, in and out of the home, and around the world. Yet when "caning," or beating described by some other euphemism, is practiced in a foreign land, many of us, including the President, become appalled, and rightly so.[16]

Paddling

Studies have shown, "That spanking can promote aggressive behavior, and hamper development of moral reasoning, reduce self-esteem and make children depressed."[17] We often seek to minimize what is in reality a barbaric practice, by using the term "paddling." But what we are doing is beating our children in their schools all across the land. Either the hand or a wooden "paddle" is usually used; and someone is called in to "witness punishment." What a performance! Euphemistic terminology does not lessen the harm we do both to the battered child and to his or her classmates who realize that a school official, who is supposedly there to teach them how to become good citizens, is striking one of their classmates. The greatest damage might well be the psychological damage done to students who are not struck, but realize what is being done to a fellow student and by whom.

Striking a child, even on the hand with a ruler, is no less intimidating than blows to the buttocks. And while it may have biblical approval, it is nonetheless an uncivilized practice that affects in some degree every member of any school where it is practiced.

If we truly want to do something about child abuse and violence, we should start in our schools. "Paddling" is no more than a euphemism for an assault; one approved by the society, and administered by public officials who should know better. In truth, if more parents would enter the fight against this form of child abuse, by orgainzing and bringing law suits, then "paddling" will go the way of the pillory and the rack.

The Fundamentalist and Violence

By referring to the biblical passage "an eye for an eye,"[18] the fundamentalist justifies his support of war and capital punishment. In so doing, he does violence to the Spirit and true beauty of the Bible.

The "eye for an eye" quotation is from the Old Testament where can be found passage after passage, previously alluded to, supporting violence as God's will in spite of some contradictory passages, such as the Commandment: "Thou shalt not kill."[19] But, generally, revenge and retribution are the hallmarks of many sections of the Old Testament, its teachings and philosophy.

The New Testament, however, introduces the teachings and philosophy of Jesus Christ for whom the Christian faith was named in A.D. 42, in the Roman province of Antioch, long after the Old Testament was written. Had the Old Testament been a true and complete revelation of God's will for mankind in the eyes of Jesus Christ, then there would have been no need for a new faith; i.e., no need for

Christianity and the New Testament. This simplistic, but at the same time profound truth, is often overlooked by the fundamentalist.

Certainly Jesus made it clear he was here to change some of the teachings of the Old Testament. For example, he said, "Ye have heard that it hath been said: An eye for an eye, and a tooth for a tooth: but I say unto you, That ye resist not evil, but whosoever shall smite thee on thy right cheek, turn to him the other also."[20]

Generally the spirit of Jesus' teachings is non-violent in nature, counseling healing, and forgiveness; a far cry from the vengeance, corporal punishment, seemingly endless imprisonments, and war that are the principal devices used in settling disputes today. He said: "For the Son of man is not come to destroy men's lives, but to save them."[21]

Then there is the cryptic biblical passage in which the Prince of Peace says: "Think not that I am come to send peace on earth: I come not to send peace but a sword."[22] But in the succeeding text, Jesus indicates he is speaking of divisive debate, not violence.

Also in seeming contradiction to his counsel against the use of force, Jesus, in the gospel of Luke, suggests his disciples buy swords.[23] His followers then show him two swords and Jesus says: "It is enough."[24] The text then goes on to indicate the swords were not viewed by Jesus as useful in settling disputes, but were to be used to fulfill prophecy regarding his subsequent arrest and crucifixion.[25]

On the use of armed force, the Bible recounts this episode: "And behold one of them which were with Jesus stretched out his hand and drew his sword, and struck a servant of the high priest's, and smote off his ear. Then said Jesus unto him. Put up again thy sword into his place: for all they that take up the sword shall perish with the sword. Thinkest thou that I cannot now pray to my Father, and he shall presently give me twelve legions of angels?"[26]

In Luke's version of this incident, Jesus is said to have touched the ear of the servant of the high priest and instantly healed him.[27] The account in the gospel of John indicates it was "Saint" Peter who struck and cut off the man's ear, and Jesus rebuked Peter for this act of violence.[28]

And on forgiveness, Jesus said: "For if ye forgive men their trespasses, your heavenly Father will also forgive you."[29] For those who were about to take his life, Jesus prayed: "Father, forgive them; for they know not what they do."[30]

And again on forgiveness: "Then came Peter to him and said, Lord, how oft shall my brother sin against me, and I forgive him? till seven times? Jesus saith unto him, I say not unto thee, until seven times: but until seventy times seven."[31]

As to the proper attitude towards one's enemies, Jesus said: "Ye have heard that it hath been said, Thou shalt love thy neighbor, and hate thine enemy. But I say unto you, Love your enemies, bless them that curse you, do good to them that hate you, and pray for them which despitefully use you, and persecute you."[32]

The Sermon on the Mount

Thomas Jefferson and others among the Founding Fathers felt obliged to reject portions of the Bible and much of the preaching of their day.[33] Jefferson used terms like "priestcraft"[34] and "slaughterhouse"[35] religion in referrng to the accretions to the teachings of Jesus and their effects on Christianity. Yet he held firmly to the belief that the unvarnished teachings of Jesus "as delivered by himself, to be the most pure, benevolent, and sublime which have ever been preached to man."[36]

Certainly one of the most liberal and beautifully written documents of all time is the Sermon on the Mount.[37] It is the jewel of the Christian faith; yet, strangely, while it meant so much to men like Jefferson, it is almost never mentioned by evangelicals and other fundamentalists. The reason, one might speculate, is that it runs squarely into the fundamentalists' conservative point of view; and although we have already touched upon several of its teachings, for emphasis, let us examine these again, together with other matters taught by Jesus in The Sermon on the Mount.

The blessed are those who are:
1. Poor in spirit[38]
2. Mourners[39]
3. Meek[40]
4. Hungering and thirsting after righteousness[41]
5. Merciful[42]
6. Pure in heart[43]
7. Peacemakers[44]

Among those who are in danger of "hell" and "the judgment" are:
1. He who hates his brother[45]
2. Those who say, "thou fool"[46]

On adultery:
" . . . whosoever looketh on a woman to lust after her hath committed adultery with her in his heart."[47]

Then comes the self-mutilation passage. Clearly a difficult one for those who claim to take the Bible literally, Jesus said:
"And if thy right eye offend thee, pluck it out, and cast it from thee for it is profitable for thee that one of thy members should perish, and not that thy whole body should be cast into hell. And if thy right hand offend thee, cut it off, and cast it from thee for it is

94

profitable for thee that one of thy members should perish, and not that thy whole body would be cast into hell."[48]

On the results of a divorce, Jesus said:
" . . . whosoever shall put away his wife, saving for the cause of fornication, causeth her to commit adultery: and whosoever shall marry her that is divorced committeth adultery."[49]

On the proper response to violence done to one's person, Jesus said:
" . . . I say unto you, That ye resist not evil but whosoever shall smite thee on thy right cheek, turn to him thy other also."[50]

If one is sued:
" . . . And if any man sue thee at the law, and take away thy coat, let him have thy cloak also."[51]

The proper response to coercion:
" . . . And whosoever shall compel thee to go a mile, go with him twain."[52]

On generosity:
"Give to him that asketh thee, and from him that would borrow of thee turn not thou away."[53]

Attitude towards one's enemies:

"Love your enemies, bless them that curse you, do good to them which dispitefully use you, and persecute you. . . ."[54]

Public display of one's religiosity:
" . . . when thou does alms, let not the left hand know what thou right hand doeth; that thine alms may be in secret; and that thy Father which seeth in secret himself shall reward thee openly. And when thou prayest, thou shall not be as the hypocrites are; for they love to stand in the corners of the streets . . . when thou prayest, enter into thy closet and when thou hast shut thy door, pray to thy Father which is in secret; and thy Father which seeth in secret shall reward thee openly."[55]

Amassing wealth:
"Lay not up for yourselves treasures upon earth, where moth and rust doth corrupt, and where thieves break through and steal: But lay up for yourself treasures in heaven, where neither moth nor rust doth corrupt, and where thieves do not break through nor steal: For where your treasure is, there will your heart be also."[56]

Diet and raiment:
" . . . Take no thought for your life, what ye shall eat, or what ye shall drink; nor yet for your body, what ye shall put on. . . . "[57]

Jesus said our attitude toward others must be decidely different from the retributive philosophy that pervades the Old Testament. He said we should "love" our enemies and "do good" to those who "hate" us. And our proper concern for those less fortunate than we are is revealed in other passages of the New Testament.

In sharp contrast, is the philosophy that seemingly guides the fundamentalist in his attitudes toward war, capital punishment; and, toward those who have broken the law, the poor, women, and those who belong to minority groups. It is an attitude reflected in the "eye for an eye, tooth for tooth, hand for hand, foot for foot, burning for burning, wound for wound, stripe for stripe" philosophy which is rampant in the Old Testament.[58]

Following the teachings of Jesus Christ is clearly not an easy thing to do; and one wonders if the hypocritical fundamentalists, who clearly do not follow the spirit of his teachings, should be called "Christians," since Jesus Christ constantly inveighed against hypocracy and distiguished his followers from "the hypocrites."[59]

From our children to world leaders, those who make mistakes should be viewed as challenges to our ability to heal. Vengeance and retribution are not sufficient healing agents to reduce our tax burdens, compensate the victims of wrongdoings, or make of the wrongdoers better, more constructive, future citizens.

As we enter the 21st century, we must emphasize healing, rebuilding, repayment, and retraining, and de-emphasize retribution, vengeance, and violence.

Societal attitudes toward wrongdoers, both domestic and international — as well as our attitude toward people generally — should be more in line with the healing, constructive; and, yes, practical spirit reflected in the Sermon on the Mount.

Notes

1. Some significant developments in the modern definition of human rights: English Bill of Rights of 1687; United States Declaration of Independence of 1776; Constitution of the United States with its Bill of Rights adoped in 1791; Treaty of Versailles that formulated the League of Nations in 1919; Kellogg-Briand Pact of 1928; Charter of the United Nations of 1945; the decisions of the Nuremberg (1945-1946) and Tokyo (1946-1948) war crimes tribunals; Genocide Convention; Inter-American Court of Human Rights; the Universal Declaration of Human Rights with the International Covenant on Civil and Political Rights and the International Covenant on Economic, Social, and Cultural rights adopted by the General Assembly in 1966; the Commission on Human Rights, under the International Covenant on Civil and Political Rights which actively conducts investigations into human rights abuses; civil rights acts of 1957, 1964, et al.; the procedures and documents leading to the creation of the European Court of Justice established in 1985.

2. Supra, note 1.

3. Declaration of Independence of the United States; July 4, 1776.

4. See: John R. Dorfman, *King of the Reform Schools Eyes Orphanages*, Wall Street Journal, February 1, 1995.

5. David Mulholland, with contribution by Wade Lambert, *Judges Finding Creative Ways of Punishing*, Wall Street Journal, May 24, 1994. See: Catherine Palmer, *Programs Help Youth and Justice Systems*, Florida Today, December 17, 1994.

6. Supra, note 5.

7. Supra.

8. See: John Adams' letter to Thomas Jefferson, January 23, 1825. Cousins, infra, p. 293; and Jefferson's notes on the *Religious Freedoms Act of 1786*; Cousins, infra, pp. 114-118.

9. See: *No Reply On Clemency In Flogging*, Los Angeles Times release appearing in Florida Today, May 4, 1994.

10. Proverbs 23:13-14.

11. Exodus 21:20-21.

12. Proverbs 10:13.

13. Proverbs 13:24.

14. Proverbs 22:15.

15. Psalms 89:32. See: Proverbs 19:18; Ezekiel 20:37; Revelation 2:27; 12:5; 19:15.

16. Supra, note 9.

17. Associated Press release from Chicago, Florida Today, January 10, 1995.

18. Exodus 21:24; Leviticus 24:20; Deuteronomy 19:21.

19. One of the Ten Commandments; Exodus 20:13.

20. Matthew 5:38. See: Matthew 5:40-48; 6:1-34; 7:1-29.

21. Luke 9:56.

22. Matthew 10:34.
23. Luke 22:36.
24. Luke 22:37-38.
25. Matthew 26:51-54.
26. Supra.
27. Luke 22:50-51.
28. John 18:10-11.
29. Matthew 6:14; Mark 11:25.
30. Luke 23:34.
31. Matthew 18:21-22. See: Mark 11:25-26; Colossians 3:13.
32. Matthew 5:43-44.
33. See: Jefferson's autobiography; Cousins, infra. pp. 118-120.
34. Jefferson's letter to Charles Clay, January 29, 1815; Cousins, supra, pp. 171-172. Also Jefferson's letter to Joseph Priestly, March 21, 1801; Cousins, supra, pp. 130-131.
35. Jefferson' letter to Thomas Whittemore, June 5, 1822; Cousins, supra, p. 158.
36. Jefferson's letter to Jared Sparks, November 4, 1820; Cousins, supra, p. 156. See: Jefferson's letter to Ezra Stiles, June 25, 1819; Cousins, supra, pp. 147-148. Jefferson's letter to Charles Thomson, January 9, 1816; Cousins, supra, pp. 145-146. Jefferson's letter to Samuel Kercheral, January 19, 1810; Cousins, supra, 139-140.
37. Matthew, chapters 5,6, and 7.
38. Matthew 5:3.
39. Matthew 5:4.
40. Matthew 5:5.
41. Matthew 5:6.

42. Matthew 5:7.

43. Matthew 5:8.

44. Matthew 5:9.

45. Matthew 5:22

46. Supra.

47. Matthew 5:28.

48. Matthew 5:29-30.

49. Matthew 5:32

50. Matthew 5:39.

51. Matthew 5:40.

52. Matthew 5:41.

53. Matthew 5:42.

54. Matthew 5:44.

55. Matthew 6:1-6.

56. Matthew 6:19-21.

57. Matthew 6:25.

58. Deuteronomy 19:21. See: Exodus 21:23-25; Leviticus 24:20.

59. Matthew 6:2,5,16. See: Matthew 7:5; 15:7; 16:3; 22:18; 23:13-14; 24:51; Mark 7:6; Luke 6:42; 11:44; 12:56; 13:15..

RESPECT FOR THE INDIVIDUAL MUST GROW

The Role of Peaceful Protest

Heraclitus was right. Eternal change is the dominant reality. As he put it, the waters continue to flow and you "cannot step in the same river twice."[1]

The increasing role of "non-elites"; i.e., the rank and file human being, in international affairs, will be the dominant force of the future. Armed with the weapons of peace and enlightenment we can take humanity to ever new heights of fulfillment. But as in the old Quaker imperative, we will have to "speak the truth to power" when it fails to recognize the innate dignity of every person.

Michael N. Nagler, drawing on the writings of Saint Augustine, believes that: "Every human life is a sacred manifestation of the macrocosm that it represents and therefore must not be willfully taken for any reason."[2] In this philosophy every person contains the essence of the totality of humankind and must, therefore, be cherished. The more we teach our children about what a human being is, and the honor and respect each life is due, the more perfect our world will be.

With such learning, gathered from the experiences of the ages and the thinking of the great philosophers, we will raise future generations that value every life, and that are far less predisposed to violence than is presently the case.

The idea that all humanity represents a single community, dates back to classical antiquity. For example, Saint Augustine wrote: "nothing we can long for or talk about, or finally get is so desireable" as this single community concept of humanity as a whole.[3] Orwell wrote the haunting line: "One life less; one world less."[4] Gandhi often quoted the Sanskrit proverb that translates: "As in the particle, so in the cosmic whole."[5]

Ultimate worth and power rests with the individual. Familes, towns, nations and world organizations are but vehicles for the expression of this power so that its full potential for creative good can be most perfectly realized. Nagler writes: "The essence of atomic technology is uniformity; every electron is like every other — which has something to do with the fact that it is an inanimate entity, or construct. No organism, no cell is exactly like any other."[6] This well illustrates the basic unity undergirding the apparent diversity in our world.

What Form of Government Is Best?

Professor Rummel says that totalitarian regimes engage in both domestic and international violence more than democracies. There have been 36 million casualties from wars in the twentieth century, and 119 million people have died through genocide, massacres, and other mass killings carried out by their own governments. Of this number, 96% were the victims of totalitarian regimes.[7]

It would seem then, at first blush, that the world suffers less at the hands of democratic leaders than from those who lead totalitarian regimes. But before we reach this conclusion, we should factor in the origin of the arms used by those who have brought about this suffering and death. When we do, and also factor in cross-border political intrigue, the blame for the human suffering in this century rests with us all: Those who made and sold armaments as well as those who used them. This is not to say that political freedom does not play a positive role in the reduction of the use of violence. This was articulated long ago by Immanuel Kant, who wrote in 1795:

"The republican constitution . . . gives a favorable prospect for the desired consequence, for example, perpetual peace. The reason is this: if the consent of the citizens is required in order to decide that war should be declared (and in this consitution it cannot but be the case), nothing is more natural than that they would be very cautious in commencing such a poor game, decreeing for themselves all the calamities of war. Among the latter would be: having to fight, having to pay the costs of wars from their own resources, having painfully to repair the devastation war leaves behind, and, to fill up the measure of evils, load themselves with a heavy national debt that would embitter peace itself and that can never be liquidated on account of constant wars in the future. But, on the other hand, in a constitution which is not republican, and under which the subjects are not citizens, a declaration of war is the easiest thing in the world to decide upon, because war does not require the ruler, who is the proprietor and not a member of the state, the least sacrifice of the pleasures of his table, the chase, his country house, his court functions, and the like. He may, therefore, resolve on war as on a pleasure party for the most trivial of reasons, and with perfect indifference leave the justification which decency requires to the diplomatic corps who are ever ready to provide it."[8]

Quincy Wright later reached essentially the same conclusion: "To sum up, it appears that absolutist states with geographically and functionally centralized governments under autocratic leadership are likely to be most belligerent, while constitutional states with geographically and functionally federalized governments under democratic leadership are likely to be most peaceful."[9]

Yet in America, slavery was not abolished until 1863; women did not get the right to vote until 1920, and it was the United States that first used nuclear weapons on open cities. In short, all types of governmental systems, including those thought to be paragons of the democratic process, make war and are capable fo horrendous acts against their own and other people. The vigilance of the masses is essential to freedom from fear, oppression, and war in any society.

Grievances in Western democracies and in Japan are usually expressed in non-violent protests, seldom in armed rebellion, for no other reason than that it is more cost effective. The cost-benefit calculus favors a non-violent approach to the redress of perceived problems. Terrorism and rebellion are considered high-risk strategies that can readily yield to more publicly supported repression than relief.[10]

The Effects of Peaceful Protests

The effectiveness of various protests in the 1950's and 60's far exceeded that of violence-oriented groups concerned with communal issues here and abroad. The Vietnam and anti-discrimination protest movements are prime examples of the worldwide effectiveness of broadly supported, non-violent protests.

The Navaho of the United States, and other native American tribes, the Maori of New Zealand, the Saami of northern Scandinavia, and the Aborigines of Australia represent indigenous people who have been adversely affected by cultural conflict with dominant societies. The Maori and Navaho, among others, because of their political effectiveness, have been able to keep some of their homelands. There are, of course, those peoples who have been removed from their native territories and forcibly taken to other lands.

The disgrace and inhumanity connected with both conquest and forcible relocation is not questioned, but there is a limit to how long old grievances can be effectively and justly reused for the purpose of repeated redress. There is a point beyond which complaints for long-past injustices become excuses for a failure to acknowledge efforts at correction and to get on with the business of building a better nation and world.

Past injustices can become a modus vivendi, stultifying creativity and the ability to successfully access the system in which one finds oneself. An organized protest should be a means to an end, not an end in itself. There is a point in which — particularly when there is the threat of violent protest — continued agitation can yield negative results, such as degrading and embarrassing paternalism. This tends to alienate some supporters, embitter many, and solve few if any long-range problems, giving only cosmetic, and temporary assistance at best.

We can all trace our lineage to another time and place. Historic hurts must not be allowed to continue to keep us from moving forward together or keep us from creating a better nation and a better world. Granted we are not yet perfect — the flawed nature of man will prevent perfection — but to allow residual discrimination to keep us from moving ahead will be tragic, as living in the past is not well suited to our moving successfully into the future.

Here in the United States a member of our largest minority has become chairman of the Joint Chiefs of Staff; another has been elected governor of Virginia; and other members of this minority have been elected mayors of some of our largest cities. The ancestors of some of these leaders were brought to our country in chains and bought and sold in our slave markets.

It is difficult, then, to show that citizens of good will of all backgrounds have not achieved, in large measure through non-violent protest, significant progress in the promotion of human rights. These citizens deserve the approbation of us all including the minorities they have helped. It should be remembered, too, that albeit they were about a hundred years late, it was the mainline churches, not the evangelical fundamentalists, that were in the forefront of this successful protest movement.

Protest Has Brought Opportunity

The United States thrives on excellence, which it often handsomely rewards. Increasingly a failure of one to receive what he feels he "deserves" may be due to his failure to prepare himself and to take advantage of the opportunities that have been opened to all since the country has become more aware of, and responsive to, the needs of its minorities. Now when flagrant discrimination does occur, legal remedies are generally available.

Competition dictates that the successful employer have the best work force he can hire. As a rule, employers want good employees no matter what their handicaps, color or ethnicity. The motivating force is not altruism but profits, and where excellence is shown it is usually rewarded, in some cases extravagantly. This is not to say that race, sex and other types of discrimination do not now exist; it is to say, that we have taken steps to eliminate all forms of discrimination, and that means of redress are now available which were not available only a relatively short time ago.

It is suggested that both nations and minorities will gain if orgainzations representing minority groups will not flag in their efforts to oppose discrimination, and at the same time strongly emphasize the need for personal excellence. A program that dwells in the past and gives only mild, if any, rebuke to incidents of violence and looting, is not well suited to do more than create frustration in the present. Needed is direction as to how to successfully access the capitalistic system devoid of subtle suggestions that violence somehow is justified by historical injustices. Minorities have proven their ability to succeed and the nation has shown, in the main, its willingness to accept and reward excellence.

What Are Minority Rights?

One can agree with Lord Acton that "the most certain test by which we judge whether a country is really free is the amount of security enjoyed by minorities."[11]

Yes, but more specifically what are minority rights? Let's have a look:

The following statement was agreed to by representatives of all the states of Eastern and Western Europe, Canada, and the United States:

"Persons belonging to national minorities have the right freely to express, preserve and develop their ethnic, cultural, linguistic or religious identity and to maintain and develop their culture in all its aspects, free of any attempt at assimilation against their will. In particular, they have the right:

-to use freely their mother tongue in private as well as in public;

-to establish and maintain their own educational, cultural and religious instititions, orgainzations or associations; . . .

-to profess and practice their religion; . . .

-to establish and maintain unimpeded contacts among themselves within their country as well as contacts across frontiers with citizens of other States; . . .

-to disseminate, have access to and exchange information in their mother tongue;

-to establish and maintain organizations within their country and to participate in international non-governmental organizations.

"Persons belonging to national minorities can exercise and enjoy their rights individually as well as in community with other members of their group."[12]

Documentation of Human Rights

The number of human rights and freedoms, recognized in various hallmark documents and legal decisions, is extensive. Some of them are: the right to life, liberty, and security of person; freedom from cruel and unusual punishment; freedom from arbitrary arrest, detension and exile; entitlement to fair and public trial; a presumption of innocence until proved guilty; privacy and the right to move freely within one's nation and internationally; freedom of exile and asylum; freedom to speak, publish, and assemble; freedom of access to public accommodations without discrimination on account of race or religion; due process of law and equal protection of the laws; full and equal citizenship; the right to vote, enforce contracts, to sue, give evidence and deal with real and personal property; equal treatment of the sexes . . . the list goes on. (For a listing of some of the landmark documents dealing with human rights, see the notes at the end of this section.)[13]

Two factors should be stressed: the Universal Declaration of Human Rights, adopted by the United Nations, speaks of "the equal rights of all members of the human family."[14] Also, the Council of Europe has adopted the European Convention for the protection of Human Rights and Fundamental Freedoms. Of great significance is the fact that it creates a court wherein individuals may bring claims against member states.[15]

It is hoped that similar world district courts will emerge in which litigants have the right of appeal to a world court, possibly the World Court at the Hague, with enforcement capabilities.

The Future Effects of Peaceful Protest

Nations will continue to express ethnic and cultural diversities, and in conflict resolution the individual should be valued above the state. As with any entity of government, the state exists as a servant of the people. There will follow a personally liberating effect, and enhanced feeling of self-esteem and self-worth, derived from elevating the underlying spiritual unity of our people in a mutual association with the whole of humanity. Human ills, rather than humans, will become the adversary in such an association of the people of the earth. As Nagler put it: "We must move toward a world in which the power to support, sustain, and to nurture will be held in higher regard than the power to destroy."[16]

War, Protest, and the Future

Nietzsche felt war enobles the human race.[17] Thomas Hobbes saw war as a part of human nature, but he believed that through government war can be abolished.[18] Thomas Aquinas contended that the use of force is justifiable to punish wrongdoers.[19]

While we should not glorify war, we must at the same time recognize it is in man's nature to do wrong occasionally and, when he does, the populace have the right to protest the wrongdoing and, if it continues, to take measure to stop the wrongdoer and bring him to trial. War and the denial of human rights are much like other human illnesses, they may require some pain to correct.

Government and law are instruments of social order necessary to the orderly functioning of our society. These tools protect our freedoms and insure our liberties at the state and local levels of our existence. They must play an increasing role in international affairs if we are to contain the diabolical weapons of modern warfare and protect the human rights of us all. The idea of an overarching authority for the protection of human rights and for the control of international violence, is not new.[20] Yet we have in place only the outline of an effectively functioning world government. Our task is to improve it.

World Leadership Accountability

We must learn to direct the use of force only at those who perpetrate injustices, and not toward innocent populations, as is also now too often the case.

As time moves on, various mutants of present-day political systems will emerge. These variations will run the gamut from the democratic to the severely totalitarian. They should not be judged by their structure, but by their treatment of people.

The challenge ahead will be to maximize human liberty and to deal effectively with those who are responsible for violations of human rights. Protests will help in this process.

At present a most glaring need is for a personal accounting by political leaders who are responsible for the violation of human rights through war or other means. Something is obviously wrong when we inflict capital punishment on ordinary citizens yet allow political leaders, who may have been responsible for the deaths of hundreds of thousands of innocent people, to retire in luxury without an accounting.

Notes

1. *Approaches to Peace, An Intellectual Map*, edited by W. Scott Thompson and Kenneth M. Jensen, with Richard N. Smith and Kimber M. Schraub; United States Institute of Peace, Washington, D.C. 1991. See: contribution by Robert Pickus, *New Approaches*, at p. 247.

2. Supra, contribution by editors, p. 372.

3. Supra, contribution by Michael N. Nagler, *Ideas of World Order and the Map of Peace*, p. 375. See: Augustine, *City of God*, XIX.11.

4. Supra, p. 379. George Orwell, *A Hanging*, in "The Collection of Essays," Journals of Letters of George Orwell, edited by Ian Angus and Sonya Orwell (London: Secker and Warburg, 1968) p. 46.

5. Supra, p. 380.

6. Supra,.p. 382

7. Supra, p. 347.

8. Supra, contribution by R.J. Rummel, pp. 352-353. Immanuel Kant, *Perpetual Peace*, translated by Lewis White Beck (New York: Library of Liberal Arts/Bobbs-Merrill, 1957) pp. 12-13.

9. Supra, contribution of R.J. Rummel, p. 364. Wright, *A Study of War*, pp. 847-848.

10. Ted Robert Gurr, *Minorities at Risk*, with contributions by Barbara Harft, Monty G. Marshall and James R. Scarritt; United States Institute of Peace, Washington, D.C., 1993, pp.

139-141. See: Jeffery Ian Ross and T.R. Gurr, *Why Terrorism Subsides: A Comparative Study of Terrorism in Canada and the United States*, Creative Politics 21 (July, 1989) pp. 405-426.

11. Supra, p. 209.

12. Supra, p. 70. U.S. Commission on Security and Cooperation in Europe, *Document of the Copenhagen Meeting of the Conference on the Human Dimension of the CSCE*; (Washington, D.C.; U.S. Government Printing Office, 1990), pp. 16-17.

13. Some significant developments in the modern definition of human rights: English Bill of Rights of 1689; United States Declaration of Independence of 1776; Constitution of the United States with its Bill of Rights adopted in 1791; Treaty of Versailles that formulated the League of Nations in 1919; Kellogg-Briand Pact of 1928; Charter of the United Nations of 1945; the decisions of the Nuremberg and Tokyo war crimes tribunals; Genocide Convention; Inter-American Court of Human Rights; the Universal Declaration of Human Rights with the International Covenant of Civil and Political Rights and the International Covenant on Economic, Social, and Cultural Rights adopted by the General Assembly in 1966; the Commission on Human Rights, under the International Covenant on Civil and Political Rights which actively conducts investigations into human rights abuses; civil rights acts of 1957, 1964, et. al.; the procedure of and documents leading to the creation of the European Community (EC) and the European Court of Justice established in 1985.

14. See: Preamble of the Universal Declaration of Human Rights.

15. Supra, note 13.

16. *Approaches to Peace*, supra, note 1.

17. Supra, p. 395.

18. Supra

19. Supra

20. Pierre Dubois (1307), Dante Alighieri (1309), Erasmus (1517), Sully (1595), Emeric Cruce (1623), Grotius (1625), William Penn (1623), Abbe de Saint-Pierre (1716), Rousseau (1761), Kant (1795). Each realized the need for a world legal and political authority. See: Robert Pickus, *New Approaches*, p. 228; *Approaches to Peace*, supra, p. 233.

THE JUST WAR THEORY

The just war theory is associated with Christianity but has its parallels in the Jewish and Islamic traditions, all being Abrahamic faiths.

Aristotle and Cicero believed a workable society was impossible without the "just" use of force. But is was not until the fourth century A.D, when Christianity became the established religion of the Roman Empire, that "Saints" Ambrose and Augustine developed the Christian just war doctrine; even though it was in opposition to passages in Deuteronomy and other Old Testament pasages sactioning the use of unbridled force in the service of God, which included the killing of children. Example: "And the Lord our God delivered him before us; and we smote him and his sons, and all his people. And we took all his cities at that time and utterly destroyed the men, and the women, and the little ones, of every city, we left none to remain."[1]

Just war advocates, while not pacifistic, as was the Christian church for the first four centuries, felt the use of force must be restrained. It was an idea that dated back through Hugo Grotius to Aristotle who had declared that to use force other than to suppress violence was not justified. He also felt that "we wage war in order to have peace,"[2] a doctrine strangely similar to the saying from the Vietnam war, "We had to destroy the village to save it."

Under the just war doctrine directly assaulting non-combatants and the taking of hostages, is prohibited. Every effort to obtain peace and to reconcile differences, without the use of force, must be tried.

Restraints on the use of force have been codified in modern times by the Geneva Conventions of 1864, 1906, and 1949 and in the Protocols of 1972 (Akehurst 1984), the Hague Regulations of 1899 and 1907, the League of Nations authorization and the charter of the United Nations. The UN charter emphasizes that force now may be used by nations, in essence, only in self-defense and that the United Nations Security Council is the ultimate legitimate authority in determining when other force may be employed among nations. Civilian protection is stressed in the first Geneva protocol. Emphasis, too, is placed on the concept that every reasonable non-violent means of conflict resolution must be employed in all cases.

But serious questions have been raised about the modern application of the just war doctrine. Many have questioned the use of force by the United States in Panama, Grenada, Nicaragua, and Haiti to preserve our hegemony in the Americas. Certainly there has been sharp criticism of the United States involvement in the Iraq-Kuwait conflict. It is agrued that the just war doctrine can and has been used to provide a rationale for the use of armed force and that the doctrine has no legitimate place in the conduct of modern international affairs.

Strangely, with all the blood-letting in the Old Testament, previously referred to, there are places where it shows a remarkable aversion to war. Warriors returning from battle were considered unclean and required atonement and purification. Even King David was told by God not to build the temple because "thou hast been a man of war, and hast shed blood"[3]; and, the ultimate messianic dream was a future time when "they shall beat their swords into plowshares, and their spears into pruninghooks: nation shall not lift up sword against nation, neither shall they learn war any more."[4]

In the Koran it is written: "and fight in the way of Allah those who fight you, but commit no aggression, for Allah does not love aggression."[5] In the Islamic tradition there is a distinction made between *jihad*, a war fought for God, and *harb*, which refers to all other kinds of warfare.[6] Islam would justify war to eliminate oppression and to protect human life, ensure freedom of religion, and to defend Islamic territories, restore homelands, and to defend against armed rebellion.[7]

Infrastructure targets such as water filtration devices have some military purpose but primarily they serve a civilian purpose. Water filtration depends on electrical grids which, too, serve a military purpose, but their destruction has a devastating effect on civilian welfare.

Therefore, in modern times with the advent of new and grotesque weapons such as nerve gas, chemical and nuclear agents, can the just war concept resonably justify the use of these weapons?

In spite of the bellicose character of fundamentalism, peaceful settlement is an authentic Christian response to the threatened and actual use of force. This is particularly true in modern times when victims of war are overwhelmingly women, children, the elderly and the environment.

The United Nations charter is squarely on the side of peace through negotiation and other non-military settlements of international crises.[8] But it can be argued that the just war doctrine tends to perpetuate and enlarge conflicts. Clearly this is the case when the doctrine is used as a rationale for the use of armed force. At one time things were clearly military or civilian related. Now bombing an airfield is far less destructive to human life than, say, the bombing of a sewer treatment plant or a power plant that serves a hospital. Increasingly the effects of modern warfare impact the civilian population and the environment.

Universal Oneness

Both science and religion point to universal elements and a mutual kinship among all people. It is in this realization that genuine spiritual and physical salvation lies rather than in making an idol of the nation-state. And it is in this realization of an inter-cosmic dependency and relationship that the one-God hypothesis finds its strongest and most compelling basis. It is found in the Sermon on the Mount and in the concept of cosmic sovereignty found in each of the Abrahamic faiths discussed.

The teachings of Jesus Christ[9] are not nationalistic but universal. He talked of the poor in spirit, the meek, the peacemakers and of suffering mankind generally. he taught in terms of all people, as did Jefferson, who said that "all men are endowed by their Creator with certain unalienable rights."[10] It is this thinking, consistent with each of the major religions, that can lead us successfully into and through the generations ahead. Yet there is the hypnotic effect of the power associated with armaments which should command our vigilance; because if it is coupled with religious fanaticism, it can destroy us.

The New Testament, Torah, and Koran, each gives ample support to non-violent conflict resolution. We must continue to learn more about each other within a framework of universal brotherhood which is consistent with the best in each of these writings.[11]

There is, for example, the powerful idea, almost identical in both Tamud and Koran, that whoever saves a single life, it is as though he saves the world.[12] It is through this idea of oneness and mutual concern that we can build a better world.

Just War as Subterfuge and Disaster

The ideas of Hugo Grotius, considered the father of modern just war thinking, have been expressed in the Hague Regulations of 1899 and 1907, in the UN charter, and in the Geneva Conventions of 1949 and the Protocols of 1977.

Yet the just war doctrine can be used as an excuse to employ gratuitous violence. All wars are "just" to high-level combatants. But there is another view: In discussing the Iraq-Kuwait conflict, Father John Langan, a Jesuit and professor of Christian ethics at Georgetown University, said that the war met the criteria of the just war doctrine, but was in reality "a catastrophe for humanity and for the peoples of the Middle East, and . . . a moral disgrace for the United States."[13] This is the attitude shared by other religious leaders including Pope John Paul II.[14] Langan points out that in modern warfare the destruction of sources of electric power, and water filtration plants, considered wonderful military achievements, have a "devastating impact" on infants, the elderly, and those people confined to institutions as well as to non-combatants generally. When one considers nuclear power, biological and chemical agents, guided missiles and other technologies, the evils inherent in modern warfare cause the just war doctrine to be seriously questioned on moral grounds. Yet a feeling of moral self-righteousness sweeps over those who feel they are fighting for the sake of God. It should be noted that in these cases political and religious leaders often promote the erroneous notion that they reflect the will of the Almighty and are led by a holy cosmic vision.

Professor Mumtaz Ahmad, of the Department of Political Science at Hampton University, indicates Muslim thinking relative to the just war doctrine by stating that war is justified first, for the elimination of oppression and the protection of human life, ensuring the free observance of religion; secondly, to defend Islamic territories against foreign aggression; thirdly, to defend and restore the rights of those who have been driven from their homes; and finally, to uphold the authority of the Islamic state against armed rebellion.[15]

False Patriotism

It should be noted here that while the "innocent non-combatant" is often used to show the injustices of war, there is another aspect of war that is often overlooked. It is the plight of those who do most of the fighting and dying. It is the plight of the ordinary soldier. Many of these, too, are essentially the innocent victims of war. They are uprooted, generally in their teen years, taken from their homes, and implicitly labeled "traitor" — even have their manhood put in question — if they fail to subject themselves to the conscription process or decline to be swayed by the jingoistic fervor of the moment. They are generally too young to effectively reason through such a complex matter. With the pressure of associates and lack of the economic wherewithal to mount an effective plea for not participating in war, they soon find themselves caught-up in the war fever of the moment, and at some far-from-home military base, one step away from combat and possible death — all not of their choosing. So many young people become unreasoning and essentially involuntary participants in war, representing human life in its prime, possibly to be sacrificed on the altar of religious and political failure. It is well to remember that the United Nations, which the radical right so strongly opposes, is squarely on the side of the non-military approach to solving the problems of national and international violence.

The sacrifice of human values to the will of the nation-state is not patriotism but idolatry which is strongly opposed by the authors of the New Testament. Monotheism implies the unity of the whole race. Salvation lies in obedience to God, not the will of the sovereign nation-state. It is accepted doctrine of all branches of Judaism, that after the Messiah comes, all sovereign states will disappear.[16]

Jean Martensen, Director of Peace Education of the Evangelical Lutheran Church of America, has said: "War is a sign of disobedience and sinfulness. War is not intended by God. All human beings are made in the image of God and they are precious and unique. Lutheran chaplains in the military with whom we have spoken have been among the most adamant of our members about war representing a failure of human imagination, a diversion of resources, in short, an incredibly sad undertaking."[17]

Again, according to Thomas Jefferson, not just the people of the United States but "all men are created equal and are endowed by their Creator with certain unalienable rights."[18] That the people everywhere should be free from oppressive government is echoed in this letter from Jefferson to James Madison in 1787: "A bill of rights is what the people are entitled to against every government on earth, general or particular; and what no just government should refuse, or rest on inference."[19]

There is a universality about the philosophy of Jefferson. Human rights were not subject to cultural and ethnic variations. As with Jesus, Jefferson constantly evidenced a concern for all men or, as we say today, all human beings in the family of mankind.

But it is difficult to expunge from our thinking the idea that the world is divided into the good people (us) and the bad people (them); that national boundaries constitute the dividing lines between the good and the bad.

The truth is, of course, that every nation has its share of both. Yet war, particularly modern wars of mass destruction, destroy indiscriminately, and the time has come to move, in the spirit of both Jesus and Jefferson, to enhance the protective powers of government at the international level of our existence, in order to bring a halt to war whether it be labeled "just" or otherwise.

Notes

1. Deuteronomy 2:33-34.
2. David R. Smock, *Religious Perspectives on War*, introduction by David Little, United States Institute of Peace Press, Washington, D.C., 1992, p. xiii.
3. First Chronicles 28:3. See: supra, note 2.
4. Isaiah 2:4; Micah 4:3;. See: supra, note 2, p. 23.
5. Supra, note 2, p. 23.
6. Supra, note 2, p. 24.
7. Supra, note 2, p. 27.
8. Charter of the United Nations, Article 1.
9. Jesus talked of the poor in spirit, the meek, the peacemakers, and suffering mankind generally. See: Matthew, chapters 5, 6, and 7, et al.
10. Declaration of Independence of the United States, 1776.
11. Supra, note 2, p. 52.
12. See: *Approaches to Peace, An Intellectual Map*, edited by W. Scott Thompson and Kenneth M. Jensen, with Richard N. Smith and Kimber M. Schraub; United States Institute of Peace, Washington, D.C., 1991: See also: contribution of Michael N. Nagler, *Ideas of World Order and the Map of Peace*, note, 33, p. 5.
13. Supra, note 2, p. 5.
14. Supra.
15. Supra, p. 27.
16. Supra, p. 46.

17. Supra, p. 51.

18. Supra, note 10.

19. *Morality and Foreign Policy*, Kenneth M. Jensen and Elizabeth P. Faulkner, editors, United States Institute of Peace, Washington, D.C., 1991. See: contribution of David Little, *Morality and National Security*, pp. 7-8.

SCHOOL PRAYERS AND FAMILY VALUES

If one believes in an omnipotent, omnicient, and omnipresent Creator,[1] then by definition God is always present and cannot be "kicked out" of the schools; an expression often used by fundamentalists in their efforts to get a prayer time inserted into the public school day. Such a Creator would also by definition, know the thoughts of our individual minds and hearts. Therefore, one's thought-prayers would be heard by such a power anytime and at any place. Thus a school student, or anyone else, can pray in their spirit anytime they wish, in school, or elsewhere, and have their prayers heard by God. This is the present situation according to practically all Christian theology.

Why then is there such a stir to have corporate, more formal and oral, prayer time in the public schools? And why confine such a time to the schools? It would be just as logical to interrupt TV and movie time, or other programming and gatherings and have a silent time or time for prayer. Instead of Mecca, Christians could face Bethlehem. Fire alarms and bells could ring at, say, noon each day to signal a cessation of all activity for a time of quiet reflection

Put in these terms, it is not difficult to see just how ridiculous and disruptive such a practice would be in our traditional day-to-day experience in the United States. It is no less ridiculous and intrusive in the day of a public school pupil. State public schools are for the teaching of basic education, but since most U.S. citizens are nominally "Christian," it is felt that while Sunday school is good, every weekday would be even better, for the implantation of "family values," as we must keep those children "moral after school."

Religion and Minorities

But Christians are not the only people with "family values." Non-believers and those of other faiths with high ethical and moral standards attend our public schools. In fairness, their beliefs should be considered, as their citizenship is no less deserving of respect than that of Christians under the First Amendment.

Yes, a student can pray in his heart anytime or place he wishes to be heard by God, according to the Bible, as we shall see later. Yet this does not satisfy the religious right. More is desired by those who promote prayer or "quiet times" for our public schools. Clearly what is desired is a foothold, a beginning at least, a first step toward religious training in the schools to recapture those supposedly lost "family values."

Sounds good and innocent enough; and, after all, what harm could it do? School officials might well like the idea of a quiet time. A minute of silence can be "heard" throughout the otherwise bustling school building and those in charge may be inclined to extend the period from, say, one minute to two, and so on. Next would come quiet meditation; a thoughtful period then developes in which the student is "permitted" to reflect . . . possibly on some school need or the misfortune of a friend or classmate.

Next, in such a scenario, would likely come the verbalized prayer; but it must be "non-proselytizing," and "non-religious," and, of course, "voluntary." Watch those words! By this time the tradition is set. The legality and traditon of a prayer time re-established and in place.

Again, why not? What's wrong with religion in the public schools? Answer: Nothing, so long as it is done evenhandedly with equal emphasis on all beliefs including the beliefs of those who are not religious; i.e. the views of both the agnostic and the atheist are given balanced consideration. What is needed is a level playing field, not a forum for expounding the teaching of the Bible only. In cases in 1962 and 1963 the Supreme Court correctly struck down officially sponsored school prayer, Bible reading, and recitation of the Lord's Prayer.[2] There is a vast difference between teaching an elective course in the great philosophies and a school-wide designated prayer service or quiet time.

Religion and Violence

Religion has a history of violence that extends to the present day. As this is being written, the great majority of "trouble spots" around the world have at their epicenters religious discord. It is a highly emotionally charged subject which easily leads to violence and hatred. We should be very careful how we proceed to use the public school system as a teaching ground for religion.

School prayer, under whatever guise, violates the most precious beliefs some people hold. These feelings vary; so that to be excused from such prayer or silent time, simply calls attention to those precious beliefs and threatens to embarrass and hold up for criticism those who do not conform in their religious beliefs to the majority view.

If we water down the silent time, then we make it essentially vapid and waste the time of the school in an area it has no business being in the first place.

But the schools are being, in many instances, manipulated by religious activists who want, in addition to purging school libraries, to have formal oral prayer or religious quiet time returned to the public schools. Even school chaplains and community lay church leaders have been suggested as school prayer directors by usually responsible sources.[3]

Zealots, and even well-meaning parents, have on occasion joined forces to turn a portion of the school's instructional time over to prayer time.

Student Initiated Prayer Time

Some public school officials have taken the position that since officially sponsored prayers are illegal, the matter could be legalized by turning it over to the students. If they wanted a prayer or silent time and voted for it, all would be legal.

But a person's religious freedom is not properly a matter of majority vote. Even a unanimous vote might include those who are intimidated and pressured to assent for fear of being considered "against God" and ostracized.

The key point here is that school prayer is a violation of the student's religious rights, which includes the right to be left alone regarding his religion even if he is a traditional Christian believer. Plebiscites, no matter how initiated, cannot legitimately alter this fact.

Even periods of silence do not constitute an academic approach to religion but are, in fact, attempts to amalgamate a highly charged set of often widely varying personal beliefs. Alloted times for prayer or silent mediation are thus an intrusion into a student's most personal life which he has every right to expect will remain inviolable while he is required to attend public school. A time set aside by school officials for quietness

135

constitutes a forfeiture of a school's responsiblity to properly manage its alloted time for the education of its students in the basic academic diciplines.

Religious neutrality is a myth. A government may try to be blind to certain religious activities and to use this supposed neutrality as a justification for its involvement in religious matters. But neutrality and blindness are not proper tests for the legitimate involvment of the state with religious training. Any involvement that promotes an established religion to the exclusion or partial exclusion of other religions and beliefs should be avoided, as religion is both a positive force and, at the same time, a potential threat to our freedoms. The complete separation of religion and government has served us well and makes each the stronger. The wall of separation should remain.[4.]

Religion is so fraught with personal emotions and beliefs as to be served best by the separation of church and state. The usual prayer conclusion, "In the name of the Father, the Son, and the Holy Ghost" threatens the very existence of the Jewish religion as a separate faith; and some Christians might well be intimidated by a failure to hear an acknowledgement of the Trinity, if this phrase is omitted from the liturgy.[5]

So let each faith proceed with its doctrinal teachings within the uninhibited confines of its own sanctuary, supported by the voluntary giving of its believers. But a public school is made up of people — usually young and impressionable — who come from highly diverse backgrounds. Any secular school will almost inevitably include, at vaious times, some non-believers. And while the public school prayer is a potential "saving ground" to some, it can be an embarrassment to others, including non-believers, and is clearly a violation of a pupil's Constitutional rights under the First Amendment.

The Role of the Fundamentalist

Why are the fundamentalists not content to let religious teaching be done in the church and home? It is because of their emphasis on what they call the Great Commission: "And he said unto them Go ye into all the world, and preach the gospel to every creature. He that believeth and is baptized shall be saved; but he that believeth not shall be damned."[6] In their effort to follow this directive, the more radical fundamentalists, which includes many sincere individuals, want to direct our thinking concerning our most personal matters; especially our sex life and our religious beliefs, in order that we will be "born again," "saved," and thus "go to heaven" . . . so they say.

Gradual Chipping

The small piece-at-a-time chipping away at the wall of separation between church and state may seem harmless. It may even seem to be a good way to bring back "lost values." Yet our nation has maintained a healthy religious heterogeneity that must be preserved.[7]

What to Do and What Not to Do

Let the church and family do the religious guidance; the schools, the academic guidance. It is a full load for each. School teachers have entirely enough collateral material to encumber their day without being caught up in the church-state separation controversy.

Values might well be revived by more insistence on civility and courtesy in the schools. Posted regulations stating the consequences of rude and abusive language, cursing the teacher, and violence should be coupled with pre-school, compulsory indoctrination sessions setting out the guidelines of conduct expected of students. Weapons, violence, and the use of pejorative terms toward teacher, officials and classmates must not be excused on the basis of cultural deprivation or ethnic diversity.

Sadly, and at the taxpayer's expense, some school systems are setting up their own police departments.[8] At best any good from this will be essentially cosmetic and temporary. Police forces do not usually generate creative thinking relative to the basic problems confronting our public school systems.

Therefore, it might ameliorate many problems to have a course dealing with the thoughts of the great thinkers as a part of the public school curriculum. This to be carefully distinguished from religious indoctrination. It would be a study in philosophy, not a devotional.

Vouchers

Voucher plans whereby the government gives to parents and/or students paper redeemable for taxpayer money by private schools, including religious schools, is clearly doing by indirection what is illegal to do directly. It is blatantly supporting denominational religious education with taxpayer dollars.

Silent Time

Periods of silence are squarely in the Quaker tradition and thus a historic form of Christian worship. The states' role is to protect freedom of religion, not to sponsor it. Yet periods of silence well suits the fundamentalist's gradualist approach to getting "prayer back in the public schools."

Another device is to allow the school to be used by religious groups, clubs, etc., either during or after school hours. Again, the school is a secular, educational institution, not a Sunday school. It is the duty of the courts to do the constitutionally correct thing and rule the government out of the religion business. While this is their duty, it may not be popular as "family values" are to many recaptureable if we will only reinstate prayer or silent time in our public schools.

The Role of the Teacher

In truth, the time spent in periods of silence and other religious activities might be better spent teaching students courtesy, respect for personal rights and just plain civility toward people in general, and toward their teachers and classmates in particular. Ethnic diversity is no excuse for a lack of manners and proper behavior toward those with whom one comes in contact in the public school system.

Prayer can involve physical as well as mental attitudes. What shall a teacher do during a "silent" time? Is he or she now to be a devotions leader? What shall be the correct demeanor for the teacher during these times? Is the teacher to sit with folded hands, bowed head, and closed eyes? Will a failure to act reverently be interpreted as being "disrespectful" of religion? Will lip movement and mumbling be allowed? Better watch that body language. Gestures like crossing oneself, may show piety rather than neutrality. If the teacher is not very careful he might be caught up in a lawsuit brought by some offended pupil and his family for violating religious freedom.[9]

As the quiet time becomes more oriented to prayer time, the temptation for the zealous teacher to proselytize may become too great to withstand. He or she might even bring a picture of Jesus to school and hang it on the wall. Not kosher said a Michigan court.[10]

Well then what about Christmas and Hanukkah, Easter and Passover? Can they be mentioned? Absolutely, if this is done in an evenhanded way.

Prayer at Graduation

What about the traditional prayer at graduation and at other school gatherings? Again, to be evenhanded, it may become necessary to have present not just the usual Protestant minister, but a Catholic cleric, a rabbi, a mufti, a witch, and ever a medicine man! It would be better to let the people do their own praying in their own way.

Student's Rights

What are the rights of the student? Clearly he cannot do what he wishes under the umbrella of religious liberty. For example, he cannot rise during class and begin to preach his faith. A public school is a restricted environment wherein a certain discipline is required for good order. The student should be permitted to bring his Bible or other

141

printed matter to school so long as his use of it does not prove disruptive.

The Student as Captive of Law and Economics

The fact that Congressional sessions are opened with prayer is often cited as a justification for having prayer time in schools. But there is a distinction to be made between the situation of a Congressman and that of a public school student.

Compulsory attendance laws and the economic condition of the student and his family often makes the choice of a private school impossible. Therefore, the student may well be in public school because he has no other resonable choice. He is not selecting a theological institution, but a public school; expecting to receive training in the basics of education. His personal religious beliefs should remain inviolable. If the student desires religious training there are churches readily available for no-cost instruction. This is the situation when the government stays out of religion.

Yet as soon as we inject a "silent" time into his public school day, we are taking from the student some of the academic time for which he is in school, imposing on teachers a burden they are not hired or prepared to handle; and, worst of all, using the "captive" student for the gratification of some perceived notions of religious fanatics bent on seeing him "saved" and on giving to him a set of religious "values." The role of government is to be the protector of a student's religious freedoms, not to be his religious mentor.

A student does not forfeit his right to show reverence in a manner of his own choosing so long as it is not distracting to or disruptive of the common enterprise of learning. To require him to either elect to be in or out of a room wherein there is reverential silence, is a violation of this First Amendment right to the "free exercise" of his religion. Clearly those who vary in their beliefs from the majority have the right not to be made by the government to feel out of place in their hearts because of their most personal religious beliefs.

Legal Action

A student made to feel uncomfortable in a prayer or silent time should be able to maintain a successful lawsuit for the violation of his religious freedoms. His case should be the stronger if he can also show he was either compelled by law to attend school or, that in order to pursue his education, he did not have the financial means to attend a non-governmentally sponsored institution.

A person's constitutional right to be left alone as to his religion and his religious practices is not the proper subject for majority vote of his fellow students. The student body has no more right to vote for school prayer time than to decide matters of budgeting, staffing, and other matters properly the function of the school's governing authority. But since they, too, are without authority to vote in a prayer period, then claiming that prayer time is a student "initiated" activity should carry no legal weight, as we have previously discussed.

Certainly students can now pray in school anytime they wish. No amendment to the Constitution, act of Congress, or legislature is needed. Parent and student alike should not want the government to set aside a time or place for their religious expressions; they should be strictly voluntary and personal in fact, as well as label.

Adding words like "nonsectarian," "non-invocational," "non-proselytizing," and "non-benedictional," to prayer or silent time authorization are but labels that do not make legal and non-invasive what is patently a violation of a person's religious liberty under the First Amendment.

The Church

In these matters the churches might consider what they are getting into by backing school prayer. Suppose a clamor arises to have all religious beliefs represented according to their traditional customs. Then chanting, dancing, drumming, mumbling, and incantations might be inserted, even insisted upon, as silence alone is a Christian tradition.

Suppose in the middle of such a quiet time a charismatic is "given" a message in tongues. Is he to stifle the spirit? Should speaking in tongues be allowed; and, if not, would such a prohibition itself at prayer times not be an abridgment of religious freedom? The troublesome possibilities are legion.

Then if these prayer times ever got to the discussion stage, what about such divisive issues as baptismal submersion, once-saved-always-saved, and other supposed requisites of "salvation."

From the perspective to the church, the doctrinal and dogmatic aspects of prayer time in the public schools might prove surprising and disappointing. The conclusion of some churches might be to try to keep formal prayer time out of the public schools and in the homes and churches of our land.

In Summation

To require a student to either stay or leave a room; i.e., to give him an option to remain with or leave his classmates for what is euphemistically called either a "quiet" time or a "prayer" time, is to put him to a spiritual election he should not be asked to make, because it is a government manipulation of his right to religious freedom under the First Amendment.

What Jesus Said

It may well be best, for those seeking a formal prayer time in the public schools, to reflect on what Jesus Christ said about the proper way to pray: "And when thou prayest, thou shall not be as the hypocrites are: for they love to pray standing in the synagogues and in the corners of the streets . . . when thou prayest, enter into thy closet, and when thou hast shut thy door, pray to thy Father which is in secret; and thy Father which seeth in secret shall reward thee openly."[11]

What the Founding Fathers Said

We will examine next, and in some detail, the opinions of our nation's Founding Fathers concerning governmental involvement in religion.

We will also see if this nation was designed to be a "Christian" nation or a nation wherein all religious beliefs would be treated equally.

Notes

1. Deuteronomy 11:12; First Kings 9:3; John 11:42; Revelation 19:6.

2. Michael D. Simpson, *School Prayer Is Back*, NEA Today, September, 1994.

3. Matthew Burke, *Chaplains For Education Front*, Wall Street Journal, January 24, 1995.

4. *"A Wall Worth Keeping*, The Economist, December 11, 1993.

5. See: note 3, supra.

6. Mark 16:15-16; See: Matthew 28:19.

7. See: note 4, supra.

8. Richard N. Ostling, *Is There A Place For God In School?*, Time, April 11, 1994.

9. Roger Rosenblatt, *Full Circle God & Country*, Family Circle, April 5, 1994.

10. Ted Gest, *The Supreme Court a Reluctant Referee*, U.S News and World Report, September 26, 1994.

11. Matthew 6:5-6.

THE UNITED STATES
WAS NOT CREATED
JUST FOR CHRISTIANS

The Founding Fathers

Suppose you were to travel to Washington, D.C. in search of evidence that the United States was created to be a Christian nation. You would find the cornerstone of our capital building, laid by George Washington, has on it words of Daniel Webster referring to "God." "In God We Trust" is on some of our money and emblazoned on the speaker's chair in the House of Representatives. Journey to the Supreme Court building and hear the crier open court with the words: "God save the United States." At the White House there is an inscription asking the blessings of heaven on its occupants. And at the very pinacle of the highest government ediface in Washington, is etched the words: "Praise Be to God," and within the Washington Monument are several quotations from the Bible.

Go next to the Library of Congress and you will see a number of Bible verses on the walls. In the National Archives building you will find "Nature's God" is mentioned in the Declaration of Independence, and "the year of our Lord" in the Constitution. Congress is opened with prayer; oaths of office, and the oath administered before testimony in court, mention the name of God. There was even a decision of the Supreme Court in 1892, while

148

not deciding the matter, that referred to our nation as being "Christian."

As if this were not enough, your pastor may tell you our nation was founded to propagate the Christian religion. If he doesn't say this, then your TV evangelist will likely do so. What, then, are you to think? Surely with so much evidence you must conclude this nation was designed to be a Christian nation.

Well, don't stop now. Keep digging. What about all those explorers and settlers kneeling in the sand bent on establishing a Christian nation. One's mind naturally pictures Columbus and the Santa Maria and the settlers at Jamestown in 1606 who wrote of "propagating the Christian religion." Their first recorded act was to erect a cross and worship. And don't forget the Mayflower Compact when, in 1620 at Plymouth, some of our forefathers wrote that they undertook their mission for the "advancement of the Christian faith." Also there is the Connecticut constitution of 1639 which says those who settled there came to "maintain and preserve the Gospel of Jesus Christ"; and don't forget the First Pennsylvania Charter of Privileges which makes reference to Jesus Christ as the "savior of the world."

So, with such overwhelming evidence, you must be convinced by now that this nation was founded by Christians, for Christians, and for the propagation of Christianity. Well, don't you believe it!

What has been left out of this piece to this point are the actions of Christians between the middle sixteen hundreds and the time the Constitution was drawn.

The mental pictures of Pilgrims at Plymouth or of an explorer wading ashore, thrusting a cross-decorated flag in the sand, represents only a part of the story. It was conditions in Europe before the settlers landed and **after** they settled here that caused the Founding Fathers concern as to the course of religious freedom in our new nation.

What about the witch-burnings in Salem? Yes, and there were other excesses. In Virginia the Church of England was established as the state church. Laws were passed prescribing horrendous punishments for those who did not toady to the religious mark.

Early settlers in Virginia continued the traditions of the Anglican Church and were intolerant of other faiths. Discrimination abounded for over 100 years. Preachers had to be licensed by the state. Citizens were fined and imprisoned for failure to support church doctrine; and in New England, scripture had been used by Calvinists in power to ban a wide variety of activities.

In the critical post-Revolutionary period, we had in our country Baptists, Presbyterians, Quakers, Mennonites, Jews, Roman Catholics,

Anabaptists, French Hugenots, Dunkers, Jesuits, Waldenes, and others — a veritable flock of denominations and creeds.

While the Founding Fathers generally resisted the biblical view of creation and attempts to legislate acceptance of ecclesiastical teachings dealing with the universe and man's role in it, their own personal creeds ranged from the Puritanism of Samuel Adams to the Deism of Paine and others. Among them it was God, yes; Jesus, yes, no, and maybe.

Thomas Jefferson in particular was concerned that religious beliefs not be entangled with government sponsorship or endorsement. The idea of enforced religion was another of his concerns. Religion was an intensely personal matter for him and those associated with him in the task of building a new nation. Ironically, the religious persecutions the settlers had fled Europe to escape had been transplanted by them in the New World. So those attending the Constitutional Convention were concerned with religious abuses that had taken place here as well as in Europe.

In Europe, Anabaptists had been burned at the stake; Quakers and Jews persecuted and killed. Tyndale had been both strangled and burned for publishing a translation of the Bible, as were some of those who dared distribute it. Puritans had been imprisoned.

In our new land, Quakers had been burned in Massachusetts. By law all "opposers of the worship of God" were declared not to be free men. This came from the very Puritans that had been persecuted themselves in Europe.

In Virginia, Baptists, Quakers, and Catholics were made unwelcome. Bail was not granted, and even the publication of Quaker beliefs brought a jail sentence. In Pennsylvania all citizens were required by law to attend church or prove they had been reading the Bible during church services.

Catholics who had found freedom in Maryland, soon lost it when Protestants came to power.

It was evident to those who gathered in Philadelphia to frame our Constitution that complete forebearance by government from the business of religion was necessary to a free people. A man's religion was between himself and his God. Religion was not government business.

Clearly the Founding Fathers believed in God. Most would even consider themselves Christian, but their brand of Christianity was not of the so-called "full gospel, charismatic, evangelical," fundamentalist variety; examples: Franklin edited the Lord's Prayer,[1] and Jefferson re-wrote the New Testament.[2] Some Founding Fathers questioned the validity of biblical miracles, and even the historicity of the life of Jesus. What these

152

young men sought was a new nation wherein there would be no government intrusions into the religious lives of its citizens.

At the particular insistance of Thomas Jefferson and James Madison, they wrote into the First Amendment: "Congress shall make no law respecting the establishment of religion, or prohibiting the free exercise thereof. . . ." The term "establishment of religion" is not resonant to the modern ear, nor do we use the word "establishment" as they did. A true feeling for what they meant by this word and the purpose behind the insertion of the First Amendment into our Constitution can be gained by understanding the religious views of its key framers and of those who set the tone for this conerstone of our religious freedom.

First, let us see what Thomas Paine thought about religion. He was probably the greatest motivator of our nation in its efforts to be rid of British rule. And we will see what Thomas Jefferson, George Washington, John Adams, Benjamin Franklin, and James Madison, thought concerning freedom of religion and learn of their feelings about the tyranical exercise of political power by religious zealots.

* * * * *

The world is my country
All mankind are my brethren,
To do good is my religion,

I believe in one God and no more.
Thomas Paine

[THOMAS PAINE: Fighter against atheism and for human freedom. Writing of what he called "the times that try men's souls," he probably did more than anyone to galvanize Americans into open defiance of British rule. George Washington said of Paine that he worked "a powerful change in the minds of many men." Andrew Jackson told a friend: "Thomas Paine needs no monument made by hands; he has erected a monument in the hearts of all lovers of liberty." Author of *Common Sense, The Age of Reason, The Rights of Man,* et al.]

Subject and Comment: **Churches Enslave and Profit**

Paine: All national institutions of churches, whether Jewish, Christian or Turkish, appear to me no other than human inventions, set up to terrify and enslave mankind, and monopolize power and profit.

I do not mean by this declaration to condemn those who believe otherwise, they have the same right to their belief as I have to mine. But it is necessary to the happiness of man that he be mentally faithful to himself. Infidelity does not consist in believing, or disbelieving; it consists in professing to believe what he does not believe.

154

It is impossible to calculate the moral mischief, if I may so express it, that mental lying has produced in society. When a man has so far corrupted and prostituted the chastity of his mind as to subscribe his professional belief to things he does not believe he has prepared himself for the commission of every other crime.[3]

* * * * *

Subject and Comment: **Out-of-Doors Church. Sabbath Day in Connecticut**

Paine: The word Sabbath, means REST; that is, cessation from labor, but the stupid Blue Laws of Connecticut make a labor of rest, for they oblige a person to sit still from sunrise to sunset on a Sabbath day, which is hard work. Fanaticism made those laws, and hypocrisy pretends to reverence them, for where such laws prevail hypocrisy will prevail also.

One of those laws says, "No person shall run on the Sabbath-day, nor walk in his garden, nor elsewhere; but reverently to and from meeting." These fanatical hypocrites forgot that God dwells not in temples made with hands, and that the earth is full of His glory.

One of the finest scenes and subjects of religious contemplation is to walk into the woods and fields, and survey the works of the God of the Creation. The wide expanse of

155

heaven, the earth covered with verdure, the lofty forest, the waving corn, the magnificent roll of mighty rivers, and the murmuring melody of the cheerful brooks, and scenes that inspire the mind with gratitude and delight.

But this the gloomy Calvinist of Connecticut must not behold on a Sabbath-day. Entombed within the walls of his dwelling, he shuts from his view the Temple of Creation. The sun shines no joy to him. The gladdening voice of nature calls on him in vain. He is deaf, dumb and blind to everything. . . .[4]

* * * * *

If men love darkness rather than light, because their works are evil, the ulcerated mind of a Calvinist, who sees God only in terror, and sits brooding over the scenes of hell and damnation, can have no joy in beholding the glories of the creation. Nothing in that mighty and wondrous system accords with his principles or his devotion.

He sees nothing there that tells him that God created millions on purpose to be damned, and that the children of a span long are born to burn forever in hell. The creation preaches a different doctrine to this. We there see that the care of goodness of God is extended impartially over all the creatures He has made. The worm of the earth shares His protection equally with the elephant of the desert. The grass that springs beneath our feet grows by his bounty as well as the cedars of Lebanon.

Everything in the creation reproaches the Calvinist with unjust ideas of God, and disowns the hardness and ingratitude of his principles. Therefore he shuns the sight of them on a Sabbath-day.[5]

* * * * *

Subject and Comment: **No Book Written by God**

Paine: All histories have been written by men. We have no evidence, nor any cause to believe, that any have been written by God. That part of the Bible called the Old Testament, is the history of the Jewish nation, from the time of Abraham, which begins i Genesis xi, to the downfall of that nation by Nebuchadnezzar, and is no more entitled to be called sacred than any other history. It is altogether the contrivance of priestcraft that has given it that name. So far from its being sacred, it has not the appearance of being true in many of the things it relates.

It must be better authority than a book which an imposter might make, as Mahomet made the Koran, to make a thoughtful man believe that the sun and moon stood still, or that Moses and Aaron turned the Nile, which is larger than the Delaware, into blood; and that the Egyptian magicians did the same. These things have too much the appearance of romance to be believed for fact.[6]

* * * * *

Subject and Comment: **Fables and Facts. Councils and Contradictions**

Paine: "Great is Diana of the Ephesians," was the cry of the people of Ephesus (Acts xix, 28); and the cry of "our holy religion" has been the cry of superstition in some instances, and of hypocrisy in others, from that day to this.

The Brahmin, the follower of Zoroaster, the Jew, the Mohometan, the Church of Rome, the Greek Church, the Protestant Church, split into several hundred contradictory sectaries, preaching in some instances damnation against each other, all cry out, "our holy religion."

The Calvinist, who damns children of a span long to hell to burn forever for the glory of God (and this is called Christianity), and the Universalist who preaches that all shall be saved and none shall be be damned (and this is also called Christianity), boast alike of their holy religion and their Christian faith.

Something more therefore is necessary than mere cry and wholesale assertion, and that something is truth; and as inquiry is the

158

road to truth, he that is opposed to inquiry is not a friend of truth.

The God of truth is not the God of fable; when, therefore, any book is introduced into the world as the Word of God, and made a groundwork for religion, it ought to be scrutinized more than other books to see if it bears evidence of being what it is called. Our reverence to God demands that we do this, lest we ascribe to God what is not His and our duty to ourselves demands it lest we take fable for fact, and rest our hope of salvation on a false foundation.

It is not our calling a book holy that makes it so, any more than our calling a religion holy that entitles it to that name. Inquiry therefore is necessary in order to arrive at the truth. But inquiry must have some principle to proceed on, some standard to judge by, superior to human authority.

When we survey the works of creation, the revolutions of the planetary system, and the whole economy of what is called nature, which is no other than the laws the Creator has prescribed to matter, we see unerring order and universal harmony reigning throughout the whole. No one part contradicts another. The sun does not run against the moon, nor the moon against the sun, nor the planets against each other. Everything keeps its apppointed time and place.

This harmony in the works of God is so obvious, that the farmer of the field, though he cannot calculate eclipses, is as sensible of it as the philosophical astronomer. He sees the God of order in every part of the visible universe.

Here, then, is the standard to which everything must be brought that pretends to be the work or Word of God, by this standard it must be judged, independently of anything and everything that man can say or do. His opinion is like a feather in the scale compared with the standard that God Himself has set up.

It is, therefore, by this standard that the Bible and all other books pretending to be the Word of God (and there are many of them in the world) must be judged, and not by the opinions of men or decrees of ecclesiastical councils. These have been so contradictory that they have often rejected in one council what they had voted to be the Word of God in another; and admitted what had before been rejected.

In this state of uncertainty in which we are, and which is rendered still more uncertain by the numerous contradictory sectaries that have sprung up since the time of Luther and Calvin, what is man to do? The answer is easy. Begin at the root — begin with the Bible itself. Examine it with the utmost strictness. It is our duty so to do.

Compare the parts with each other, and the whole with the harmonious, magnificent order that reigns throughout the visible universe, and the result will be, that if the

160

same Almighty wisdom that created the universe dictated also the Bible, the Bible will be as harmonious and as magnificient in all its parts and in the whole as the universe is.

But, if instead of this, the parts are found to be discordant, contradicting in one place what is said in another (as in II Sam xxiv, I, and I Chron. xxi, I, where the same action is ascribed to God in one book and to Satan in the other), abounding also in idle and obscene stories, and representing the Almighty as a passionate, whimsical Being, continually changing His mind, and making and unmaking His own works as if he did not know what he was about, we may take it for certainty that the Creator of the Universe is not the author of such a book, that it is not the Word of God, and that to call it so is to dishonor His name.

The Quakers, who are a people more moral and regular in their conduct than the people of other sectaries, and generally allowed so to be, do not hold the Bible to be the Word of God. They call it a history of the times, and a bad history it is, and also a history of bad men and of bad actions, and abounding with bad examples.[7]

* * * * *

Subject and Comment: **Reason and the Word of God**

Paine: . . . my endeavors have been directed to bring man to a right use of the reason that God has given him; to impress on him the great principles of divine morality, justice, and mercy, and a benevolent disposition to all men, and to all creatures; and to inspire in him a spirit of trust, confidence and consolation, in his Creator, unshackled by the fables of books pretending to be the word of God.[8]

* * * * *

Subject and Comment: **Deism and Bibles**

Paine: Deism then teaches us, without the possibility of being deceived, all that is necessary or proper to be known. The creation is the Bible of the Deist. He there reads, and in the hand-writing of the Creator himself, the certainty of his existence, and the immutability of his existence, and the immutability of his power; and all other Bibles and Testaments are to him forgeries.[9]

* * * * *

Subject and Comment: **Revelation and Detestable Wickedness**

Paine: Though, speaking for myself, I admit the possibility of revelation, I totally disbelieve that the Almighty ever did

162

communicate any thing to man, by any kind of vision, or appearance, or by any means which our senses are capable of receiving, otherwise than by the universal display of himself in the works of the creation, and by that repugnance we feel in ourselves to bad actions, and dispositions to good ones.

The most detestable wickedness, the most horrid cruelties, and the greatest miseries, that have afflicted the human race, have had their origin in this thing called revelation, or revealed religion. It has been the most dishonorable belief against the character of the divinity, the most destructive to morality, and the peace and happiness of man, that ever was propagated since man began to exist.[10]

* * * * *

Subject and Comment: **Bible Stories**

Paine: If these stories are false we err in believing them to be true, and ought not to believe them. It is therefore a duty which every man owes to himself, and reverentially to his Maker, to ascertain by every possible inquiry whether there be a sufficient evidence to believe them or not.

My own opinion is, decidedly, that the evidence does not warrant the belief, and that we sin in forcing that belief upon ourselves and upon others.[11]

* * * * *

Subject and Comment: **Contradictory Character of Creator as Portrayed in Bible**

Paine: When we reflect on a sentence so tremendously severe as that of consigning the whole human race, eight persons excepted, to deliberate drowning; a sentence, which represents the Creator in a more merciless character than any of those who we call Pagans ever represented the Creator to be under the figure of any of their deities, we ought at least to suspend our belief of it, on a comparison of the beneficent character of the Creator with the tremendous severity of the sentence; but when we see the story told with such evident contradiction of circumstances, we ought to set it down for nothing better than a Jewish fable told by nobody knows whom and nobody knows when.[12]

* * * * *

Had it come to us as an Arabic or Chinese book, and said to have been a sacred book by the people from whom it came, no apology would have been made for the confused and disordered state it is in. The tales it related of the Creator would have been censured, and our pity excited for those who believed them. We should have vindicated the goodness of

164

God against such a book, and preached up the disbelief of it out of reverence to Him. . . .[13]

* * * * *

It is therefore necessary that the book be examined; it is our duty to examine it; and to suppress the right of examination is sinful in any government, or in any judge or jury. The Bible makes God to say to Moses, Deut. vii. 2, "And when the Lord thy God shall deliver them before thee, thou shalt smite them, and utterly destroy them, thou shalt make no covenant with them, nor show mercy unto them."

Not all priests, nor scribes, nor tribunals in the world, nor all the authority of man, shall make me believe that God ever gave such a Roseperrian precept as that of showing no mercy; and consequently it is impossible that I or any person who believes as reverentially of the Creator as I do can believe such a book to be the Word of God.[14]

* * * * *

Subject and Comment: **Lasciviousness, Debauchery, and Infidelity**

Paine: Religion is a private affair between every man and his Maker, and no tribunal or third party has a right to interfere between them. It is not properly a thing of this world;

it is only practiced in this world; but its object is in a future world; and it is not otherwise an object of just laws than for the purpose of protecting the equal rights of all, however various their belief may be.

If one man choose to believe the book called the Bible to be the Word of God, and another, from the convinced idea of the purity and perfection of God compared with the contradictions the book contains, from the lasciviousness of some of its stories, like that of Lot getting drunk and debauching his two daughter, which is not spoken of as a crime, and for which the most absurd apologies are made — from the immorality of some of its precepts, like that of showing no mercy — and from the total want of evidence on the case — thinks he ought not to believe it to be the Word of God, each of them has an equal right; and if the one has a right to give his reasons for believing it to be so, the other has an equal right to give his reasons for believing the contrary.[15]

* * * * *

Subject and Comment: **God Reflected in Universe**

Paine: Contemplating the universe, the whole system of Creation, in this point of light, we shall discover, that all that which is called natural philosophy is properly a devine study.

It is the study of God through His works. It is the best study, by which we can arrive at a knowledge of His existence, and the only one by which we can gain a glimpse of His perfection.[16]

* * * * *

Subject and Comment: **The Support of Priestcraft**

Paine: The words revealed religion and natural religion also require explanation. They are both invented terms, contrived by the Church for the support of its priestcraft. With respect to the first, there is no evidence of any such thing, except in the universal revelation that God has made of His power, His wisdom, His goodness, in the structure of the universe, and in all the works of creation.

We have no cause for ground from anything we behold in those works to suppose that God would deal partially by mankind, and reveal knowledge to one nation and withhold it from another, and then damn them for not knowing it. The sun shines an equal qantity of light all over the world — and mankind in all ages and countries are endued with reason and blessed with sight, to read the visible works of God in the creation, and so intelligent is the book that he that runs may read.[17]

* * * * *

Man has the power of making books,
inventing stories of God, and call them
revelation, or the Word of God. The Koran
exists as an instance that this can be done,
and we must be credulous indeed to support
that this is the only instance and Mahomet
the only imposter. The Jews could match him,
and the Church of Rome could overmatch the
Jews. The Mahometans believe the Koran, the
Christians believe the Bible, and it is
education [that] makes all the difference.

Books, whether Bibles or Korans, carry no
evidence of being the work of any other
power than man. It is only that which man
cannot do that carries the evidence of being
the work of a superior power. Man could not
invent and make a universe — he could not
invent nature, for nature is of divine origin. It
is the laws by which the universe is
governed.[18]

* * * * *

Subject and Comment: **Delusion and
Falsehood in the Bible**

Paine: Delusion and falsehood cannot be
carried˙higher than they are in this passage.
You, Sir, are but a novice in the art. The words
admit of no equivocation. The whole passage
is in the first person and the present tense,

168

"We which are alive." [Ed. See: First Thessolonians 4:17.]

Had the writer meant a future time, and a distant generation, it must have been the third person and the future tense. "They who shall then be alive." I am thus particular for the purpose of nailing you down to the test, that you may not ramble from it, nor put other constructions upon the words than they will bear, which priests are very apt to do.

Now, Sir, it is impossible for serious man, to whom God has given the divine gift of reason, and who employs that reason to reverence and adore the God that gave it, it is, I say, impossible for such a man to put confidence in a book that abounds with fable and falsehood as the New Testament does. This passage is but a sample of what I could give you.[19]

* * * * *

[**Thomas Jefferson:** Generally admired by those of both current major parties in the United States and great numbers of freedom-loving people throughout the rest of the world. Author of the Declaration of Independence; third President of the United States; father of the University of Virginia.]

Subject and Comment: **We Persecuted Our Own People**

Jefferson: The first settlers in this country were emigrants from England, of the English church, just at a point of time when it was flushed with complete victory over the religions of all other persuasions. Possessed, as they became, of the powers of making, administering, and executing the laws, they showed equal intolerance in this country with their Presbyterian brethern, who had emigrated to the northern government. The poor Quakers were flying from persecution in England. They cast their eyes on these new countries as asylums of civil and religious freedom; but they found them free only for the reigning sect. Several acts of the Virginia Assembly of 1659, 1662, and 1663, had made it penal in parents to refuse to have their children baptized; had prohibited the unlawful assembling of Quakers; had made it penal for any master of a vessel to bring a Quaker into the state; had ordered those already here, and such as should come hereafter to be imprisoned until they should abjure the country; provided a milder punishment for their first and second return, but death for their third; had inhibited all persons from suffering their meeting in or near their houses, entertaining them individually, or disposing of books which supported their tenets.

If no executions took place here as did in New England, it was not owing to the moderation of the church, or spirit of the legislature, as may be inferred from the law itself; but to historical circumstances which have not been handed down to us. The Anglicans retained full possession of the country about a century. Other opinions began then to creep in, and the great care of the government to support their own church, having begotten an equal degree of indolence in its clergy, two-thirds of the people had become dissenters at the commencement of the present revolution. The laws, indeed, were still oppressive on them, but the spirit of the one party had subsided into moderation, and the other had risen to a degree of determination which commanded respect.

The present state of our laws on the subject of religion is this. The Convention of May, 1776, in their declaration of rights, declared it to be a truth, and a natural right, that the exercise of religion should be free; but when they proceeded to form on that declaration the ordinance of government, instead of taking up every principle declared in the bill of rights, and guarding it by legislative sanction, they passed over that which asserted our religious rights, leaving them as they found them. The same convention, however, when they met as a member of the general assembly in October, 1776, repealed all acts of Parliament which had rendered criminal the maintaining any opinions in matters of religion, the forebearing to repair to church, and the exercising any mode of worship; and suspended the laws giving salaries to the clergy, which suspension was made perpetual in October, 1779. Statutory oppression in religion being thus wiped away, we remain at present under those only imposed by the common laws, or by our own acts of assembly. At the common law, heresy was a capital offense, punishable by burning. Its definition was left to the ecclesiastical judges, before whom conviction was, till the statute of I.El.c.I circumscribed it, by declaring, that nothing should be deemed heresy, but what had been so determined by authority of the canonical scriptures or by one of the four first general councils, or by other council having for grounds of their declaration the express and plain words of the scriptures. Heresy, thus circumscribed, being an offense at the common law, our act of assembly of October, 1776, c. 17, gives cognizance of it to the general court, by declaring that the jurisdiction of that court shall be general in all matters of common law. The execution is by writ *De hoeretico comburendo* [On the Burning of a Heretic]. By our own act of assembly of 1705, c. 30, if a person brought up in the Christian religion denies the being of a God, or the Trinity, or asserts there are more gods than one, or denies the Christian religion to be true, or the scriptures to be of divine authority, he is punishable on the first offense by incapacity to hold any office or employment ecclesiastical, civil or military; on the second by disability to sue, to take any gift or legacy, to be guardian, executor, or administrator, and by three years imprisonment without bail. A father's right to the custody of his own children being founded in law on this right to guardianship, this being taken away, they may of course be severed from him, and put by the authority of the court into more orthodox hands.

This is a summary view of that religious slavery, under which a people have been willing to remain, who have lavished their lives and fortunes for the establishment of their civil freedom. The error seems not sufficiently eradicated, that the operations of the mind, as well as the acts of the body, are subject to the coercion of the laws. But our rulers can have no authority over such natural rights, only as we have submitted to them. The rights of conscience we never submitted, we could not submit. We are answerable for them to our God. The legitimate powers of government extend to such acts only as are injurious to others. But it does me no injury for my neighbor to say there are twenty Gods, or no God. It neither picks my pocket nor breaks my leg.[20]

* * * * *

The bill for establishing religious freedom, the principles of which had, to a certain degree, been enacted before, I had drawn in all latitude of reason and right. It still met with opposition; but, with some mutilations in the preamble, it was finally passed; and a singular proposition proved that its protection of opinion was meant to be universal. Where the preamble declares, that coercion is a departure from the plan of the holy author of our religion, an amendment was proposed, by inserting the word "Jesus Christ" so that it should read, "a departure from the plan of Jesus Christ, the holy author of our religion"; the insertion was rejected by a great majority, in proof that they meant to comprehend, within the mantle of its protection, the Jew and the Gentile, the Christian and the Mohometan, the Hindoo, and the Infidel of every denomination.[21]

* * * * *

Subject and Comment: **Human Mind Freed from Vassalage**

Jefferson: The Virginia act for religious freedom has been received with infinite approbation in Europe, and propagated with enthusiasm. I do not mean by the governments, but by the individuals who compose them. It has been translated into French and Italian, has been sent to most of the courts of Europe, and has been the best evidence of the falsehood of those reports which stated us to be in anarchy. It is inserted in the new Encyclopedie, and is appearing in most of the publications respecting America. In fact, it is comfortable to see the standard of reason at length erected after so many ages, during which the human mind has been held in vassalage by kings, priests, and nobles; and it is honorable for us, to have produced the first legislature who had the courage to declare, that the reason of man may be trusted with the formation of his own opinions.[22]

* * * * *

Subject and Comment: **Hands of Power**

Jefferson: What an effort, my dear sir, of bigotry in politics and religion have we gone through! The barbarians really flattered themselves they should be able to bring back the times of vandalism when ignorance put everything into the hands of power and priestcraft.[23]

* * * * *

Subject and Comment: **Religion Lies Solely Between Man and God**

Jefferson: Believing with you that religion is a matter which lies solely between man and his God, that he owes account to none other for his faith or his worship, that the

175

legislative powers of government reach actions only, and not opinions, I contemplate with sovereign reverence that act of the whole American people which declared that their legislature should "make no law respecting an establishment of religion, or prohibiting the free exercise thereof," thus building a wall of separation between Church and State.[24]

* * * * *

Subject and Comment: **Priests as Enemies of the Mind**

Jefferson: An opposition, in the meantime, has been got up. That of our alma mater, William and Mary, is not of much weight. She must descend into the secondary rank of academies of preparation for the University. The serious enemies are the priests of the different religious sects, to whose spells on the human mind its improvement is ominous. Their pulpits are now resounding with denuciations against the appointment of Dr. Cooper, whom they charge as a monotheist in oppositon to their tritheism. Hostile as these sects are, in every other point, to one another they unite in maintaining their mystical theology against those who believe there is one God only. The Presbyterian clergy are loudest; and most intolerant of all sects, the most tyrannical and ambitious; ready at the word of the lawgiver, if such a word could be now obtained, to put the torch to the pile, and to rekindle in this virgin hemisphere, the flames in which their oracle Calvin consumed the poor Servetus, because he could not find in his Euclid the proposition which had demonstrated that three are one and one is three, nor subscribed to that of Calvin, that magistrates have a right to exterminate all heretics to Calvinistic Creed. They pant to re-establish, by law, that holy inquisition, which they can now only infuse into public opinion. We have most unwisely committed to the hierophants of our particular superstition, the direction of public opinion, that lord of the universe. We have given them stated and privileged days to collect and catechise us, opportunities of delivering their oracles to the people in mass, and of moulding their minds as wax in the hollow of their hands.[25]

* * * * *

Subject and Comment: **Religious Creeds Bane and Ruin of Christian Church. They Have Made of Christendom a Slaughterhouse**

Jefferson: Your asked my opinion on the items of doctrine in your catechism. I have never permitted myself to meditate a specific creed. These formulas have been the bane and ruin of the Christian church, its own fatal

177

invention, which, through so many ages, made of Christendom a slaughter-house, and at this day divides it into casts of inextinguishable hatred to one another.[26]

* * * * *

Subject and Comment: **Question God, Jesus, and Miracles. Avoid Servile Crouching**

Jefferson: Religion. Your reason is now mature enough to examine this object. In the first place, divest yourself of all bias in favor of novelty and singularity of opinion. Indulge them in any other subject rather than that of religion. It is too important, and the consequences of error may be too serious. On the other hand, shake off all the fears and servile prejudices, under which weak minds are servilely crouched. Fix reason firmly in her seat, and call to her tribunal every fact, every opinion. Question with boldness even the existence of a God; because, if there be one, he must more approve of the homage of reason, than that of blindfolded fear.

You will naturally examine first the religion of your own country. Read the Bible, then, as you would read Livy or Tacitus. The facts which are within the ordinary course of nature, you will believe on the authority of the writer, as you do those of the same kind in Livy and Tacitus. The testimony of the writer weights in their favor, in one scale, and their not being against the laws of nature, does not weigh against them. But those facts in the Bible which contradict the laws of nature, must be examined with more care, and under a variety of faces. Here you must recur to the pretensions of the writer to inspiration from God. Examine upon what evidence his pretensions are founded, and whether that evidence is so strong, as that its falsehood would be more improbable than a change in the laws of nature, in the case he relates. For example, in the book of Joshua, we are told the sun stood still several hours. Were we to read that fact in Livy or Tacitus, we should class it with their showers of blood, speaking of statutes, beasts, etc. But it is said, that the writer of that book was inspired. Examine, therefore, candidly, what evidence there is of his having been inspired. The pretension is entitled to your inquiry, because millions believe it. On the other hand, you are astronomer enough to know how contrary it is to the law of nature that a body revolving on its axis, as the earth does, should have stopped, should not, by that sudden stoppage, have prostrated animals, trees, buildings, and should after a certain time have resumed its revolution, and that without a second general prostration. Is this arrest of the earth's motion, or the evidence which affirms it, most within the law of probabilities?

You will next read the New Testament. It is the history of a personage called Jesus.

179

Keep in your eye the opposite pretensions: 1, of those who say he was begotten of God, born of a virgin, suspended and reversed the laws of nature at will, and ascended bodily into heaven; and 2, of those who say he was a man of illegitimate birth, a benevolent heart, enthusiastic mind, who set out without pretensions of divinity, ended in believing them, and was punished according to the Roman law, which punished the first commission of that offense by whipping, and the second by exile, or death, *in furea..* See this law in the Digest, Lib. 48. tit. 19. S28.3 and Lipsius Lib. 2 de cruce. cap. 2.

These questions are examined in the books I have mentioned, under the head of Religion, and several others. They will assist you in your inquires; but keep your reason firmly on the watch in reading them all.

Do not be frightened from this inquiry by any fear of its consequences. If it ends in a belief that there is no God, you will find incitements to virtue in the comfort and pleasantness you feel in its exercise, and the love of others which it will procure you. If you find reason to believe there is a God, a consciousness that you are acting under his eye, and that he approves you will be a vast additional incitement; if that there be a future state, the hope of a happy existence in that increases the appetite to deserve it; if that Jesus was also a God, you will be comforted by a belief of his aid and love.

In fine, I repeat, you must lay aside all prejudice on both sides, and neither believe nor reject anything because any other person, or description of persons, have rejected it or believed it. Your own reason is the only oracle given you by heaven, and you are answerable, not for this rightness, but the uprightness of the decision.

I forgot to observe, when speaking of the New Testament, that you should read all the histories of Christ, as well as those whom a council of ecclesiastics have decided for us, to be Pseudo-evangelists as those they named Evangelists. Because these Pseudo-evangelists pretend to inspiration, as much as the others, and you are to judge their pretensions by your own reason, and not by the reason of those ecclesiastics. Most of these are lost. There are some, however, still extant, collected by Fabricius, which I will endeavor to get and send to you.[27]

* * * * *

Subject and Comment: **All Religions Agree on Some Basic Points**

Jefferson: Reading, reflection and time have convinced me that the interests of society require the observation of those moral precepts only in which all religions agree (for all forbid us to murder, steal, plunder, or bear false witness) and that we should not intermeddle with the particular dogmas in which all religions differ, and which are totally unconnected with morality.[28]

* * * * *

Subject and Comment: **The Real Anti-Christ**

Jefferson: Nothing is more exactly and seriously true than what is there stated; that but a short time elapsed after the death of the great reformer of the Jewish religion, before his principles were departed from by those who professed to be his special servants, and perverted into an engine for enslaving mankind, and aggrandizing their oppressors in Church and state; that the purest system of morals ever before preached to man has been adulterated and sophisticated by artificial constructions, into a mere contrivance to filch wealth and power to themselves; that rational men, not being able to swallow their impious heresies, in order to force them down their throats, they raise the hue and cry of infidelity, while themselves are the greatest obstacles to the advancement of the real doctrine of Jesus, and do, in fact, constitute the real Anti-Christ.[29]

* * * * *

Subject and Comment: **Don't Let Subtleties and Mysteries Confuse. All Good Men His Children**

Jefferson: An eloquent preacher of your religious society, Richard Motte, in a discourse of much emotion and pathos, is said to have exclaimed aloud to his congregation, that he did not believe there was a Quaker, Presbyterian, Methodist, or Baptist in heaven, having paused to give his hearers time to stare and to wonder. He added, that in Heaven, God knew no distinctions, but considered all good men as his children, and as brethren of the same family.

I believe with the Quaker preacher, that he who steadily observes those moral precepts in which all religions concur, will never be questioned at the gates of heaven, as to the dogmas in which they all differ. That on entering there, all those are left behind us, and the Aristides and Catos, and Penns and Tillotsons, Presbyterians and Baptists, will find themselves united in all principles which are in concert with the reason of the supreme mind.[30]

* * * * *

Subject and Comment: **No Denominations in Heaven**

Jefferson: Our particular principles of religion are a subject of accountability to our God alone. I inquire after no man's, and trouble none with mine; nor is it given to us in this life to know whether yours or mine, our friends or our foes, are exactly the right. Nay, we have heard it said that there is not a Quaker or a Baptist, a Presbyterian or an Episcopalian, a Catholic or a Protestant in heaven; that on entering that gate, we leave those badges of schism behind and find ourselves united in those principles only in which God has united us all. Let us not be uneasy then about the different roads we may pursue, as believing them the shortest, to that our last abode; but, following the guidance of a good conscience, let us be happy in the hope that by these different paths we shall all meet and embrace, is my earnest prayer.[31]

* * * * *

Subject and Comment: **Crazy Theologists**

Jefferson: No doctrines of his [Jesus'] lead to schism. It is the speculations of crazy theologists which have made a Babel of a religion the most moral and sublime ever preached to man, and calculated to heal, and not to create differences. These religious animosities I impute to those who call themselves his ministers, and who engraft their casuistries on the stock of his simple precepts. I am sometimes more angry with them than is authorized by the blessed charities which he preaches.[32]

* * * * *

Subject and Comment: **Separate Gold from Dross**

Jefferson: Among the sayings and discourses imputed to him [Jesus] by his biographers, I find many passages of fine imagination, correct morality, and of the most lovely benevolence; and others, again, of so much ignorance, so much absurdity, so much untruth, charlatanism and imposture, as to pronounce it impossible that such contradictions should have preceeded from the same being. I separate, therefore, the gold from the dross. . . .[33]

* * * * *

It is surely time for men to think for themselves, and to throw off the authority of names so artifically magnified . . . I say, that his free exercise of reason is all I ask for the vindication of the character of Jesus. We find in the writings of his biographers matter of two distinct descriptions. First, a groundwork of vulgar ignorance, of things impossible, of superstitions, fanaticisms, and fabrications.

Intermixed with these, again, are sublime ideas of the Supreme Being, aphorisms, and precepts of the purest morality and benevolence, sanctioned by a life of humility, innocence and simplicity of manners, neglect of riches, absence of worldly ambitions and honors, with an eloquence and persuasiveness which have not been surpassed.[34]

* * * * *

Subject and Comment: **Trinitarian Arithmetic. Mysteries, Fancies, and Falsehoods**

Jefferson: When we shall have done away with the incomprehensible jargon of the Trinitarian arithmetic, that three are one, and one is three; when we shall have knocked down the artificial scaffolding, reared to mask from view the simple structure of Jesus; when, in short, we shall have unlearned everything which has been taught since his day and get back to the simple doctrines he inculcated, we shall then be truly and worthily his disciples; and my opinion is that if nothing had ever been added to what flowed purely from his lips, the whole world would at this day have been Christian.[35]

* * * * *

186

Subject and Comment: **Don't You Just Love Jesus?**

Jefferson: In our Richmond there is much fanaticism, but chiefly among the women. They have their night meetings and praying parties, where, attended by their priests, and sometimes by a hen-pecked husband, they pour forth the effusions of their love of Jesus, in terms as amatory and carnal, as their modesty would permit them to use to a mere earthly lover.[36]

* * * * *

Subject and Comment: **Authors of New Testament**

Jefferson: To do him [Jesus] justice, it would be necessary to remark the disadvantages his doctrines had to encounter, not having been committed to writing himself, but by the most unlettered of men, by memory, long after they had heard them from him; and presented in every paradoxical shape.[37]

* * * * *

Subject and Comment: **Jeffersonian Christianity**

Jefferson: I am a Christian in the only sense in which I believe Jesus wished anyone to be, sincerely attached to his doctrine in preference to all others; ascribing to him all human excellence, and believing that he never claimed any other.[38]

* * * * *

Subject and Comment: **Mystical Generation of Jesus**

Jefferson: And the day will come, when the mystical generation of Jesus, by the Supreme Being as his father, in the womb of a virgin, will be classed with the fable of the generation of Minerva in the brain of Jupiter.[39]

* * * * *

Subject and Comment: **Of Priests and Infidels; Pence and Power**

Jefferson: By the same test the world must judge me. But this does not satisfy the priesthood. They must have a positive, a declared assent to all their interested absurdities. My opinion is that there would never have been an infidel, if there had never been a priest. The artificial structures they have built on the purest of all moral systems, for the purpose of deriving from it pence and power, revolts those who think for themselves, and who read in that system only what is really there. These, therefore, they brand with such nick-names as their enmity chooses gratuitously to impute.[40]

* * * * *

Subject and Comment: **Bigotry a Disease of Ignorance**

Jefferson: Bigotry is the disease of ignorance, of morbid minds; enthusiasm of the free and buoyant. Education and free discussion are the antidotes of both.[41]

* * * * *

[**George Washington:** The cohesive force ideally suited to preside at the Constitutional Convention; and, later, his prestige was of great value in getting the Constitution radified. Although he had only five years of formal schooling, he became our first President, and came to be called "The Father of His Country."]

Subject and Comment: **Everyman's Vine and Fig Tree**

Washington: It would be inconsistent with the frankness of my character not to avow that I am pleased with your favorable opinion of my administration, and fervent wishes for my felicity. May the Children of the Stock of

189

Abraham, who dwell in this land, continue to merit and enjoy the good will of other inhabitants, while every one shall sit in safety under his own vine and fig-tree, and there shall be none to make him afraid. May the father of all mercies scatter light and not darkness in our paths, and make us all in our several vocations useful here, and in his own due time and way everlastingly happy.[42]

* * * * *

Subject and Comment: **Truth Over Bigotry and Superstition**

Washington: We have abundant reason to rejoice that in this Land the light of truth and reason has triumphed over the power of bigotry and superstition, and that every person may here worship God according to the dictates of his own heart. In this enlightened Age and in this Land of equal liberty it is our boast, that a man's religious tenets will not forfeit the protection of the Laws, nor deprive him of the right of attaining and holding the highest Offices that are known in the United States.

Your prayers for my present and future felicity are received with gratitude; and I sincerely wish, Gentlemen, that you may in your social and individual capacities taste those blessings which a gracious God bestows upon the Righteous.[43]

190

* * * * *

Subject and Comment: **Acrimony and Irreconcilable Hatreds**

Washington: I have now before me your letters of the 9 January and 12 of February to which it will not be in my power to reply so fully as my inclination would lead me to do if I had no avocation but those of a personal nature.

I regret exceedingly that the disputes between the Protestants and Roman Catholics should be carried to the serious alarming height mentioned in your letters. Religious controversies are always productive of more acrimony and irreconcilable hatreds than those which spring from any other cause; and I was not without hopes that the enlightened and liberal policy of the present age would have put an effectual stop to contentions of this kind.[44]

* * * * *

[**John Adams:** His ideas influenced Jefferson, and were reflected in the Declaration of Independence. Adams served in the Continental Congress. He was the second President of the United States, and father of John Quincy Adams, our sixth President.]

Subject and Comment: **Frightful Engines and Ecclesiastical Councils**

Adams: The frightful engines of ecclesiastical councils, of diabolical malice and Calvinistic good-nature never failed to terrify me exceedingly whenever I thought of preaching. But the point is now determined and I shall have liberty to think for myself without molesting others or being molested myself. Write to me the first good opportunity, and tell me freely whether you approve my conduct.[45]

* * * * *

Subject and Comment: **Most Bloody Religion, and Millions of Fables**

Adams: Christianity, you will say, was a fresh revelation. I will not deny this. As I understand the Christian religion, it was, and is, a revelation. But how has it happened that millions of fables, tales, and legends, have been blended with both Jewish and Christian revelation that have made them the most bloody religion that ever existed?[46]

* * * * *

Subject and Comment: **Man's Hand in the Word of God**

Adams: What havoc has been made of books through every century of the Christian era? Where are fifty gospels condemned as spurious by the bull of Pope Gelasius? Where are the forty wagon-loads of Hebrew manuscripts burned in France, by order of another pope because suspected of heresy? Remember the index expurgatorius, the inquisition, the stake, the axe, the halter, and the guillotine; and, oh, horrible, the rack? This is as bad, if not worse, than a slow fire. Nor should the Lion's Mouth be forgotten.[47]

* * * * *

Subject and Comment: **The Word of God?**

Adams: Aristotle wrote the history of eighteen hundred republics which existed before his time. Cicero wrote two volumes of discourses on government, which, perhaps, were worth all the rest of his works. The works of Livy and Tacitus, &c., that are lost, would be more interesting than all that remain. Fifty gospels have been destroyed, and where are Luke's world of books that have been written? If you ask my opinion who has committed all the havoc, I will answer candidly, — Ecclesiastical and Imperial despotism has done it to conceal their frauds.[48]

* * * * *

Subject and Comment: **The Trinity?**

193

Adams: The human understanding is a revelation from its Maker, which can never be disputed or doubted. There can be no scepticism, Pyrrhonism, or incredulity or infidelity here. No prophecies, no miracles are necessary to prove this celestial communication. The revelation has made it certain that two and one make three, and that one is not three nor can three be one. We can never be so certain of any prophecy, or the fulfillment of any prophecy, or of any miracle, or the design of any miracle, as we are from the revelation of nature, this is Nature's God, that two and two are equal to four. Miracles or prophecies might frighten us out of our wits: might scare us to death; might induce us to lie, to say that we believe that two and two make five. But we should not believe it. We should know the contrary.

Had you and I been forty days with Moses on Mount Sinai, and admitted to behold the divine Shekinah, and there told that one was three and three one, we might not have had the courage to deny it, but we could not have believed it. The thunders and lightnings, and earthquakes, and the transcendent splendors and glories might have overwhelmed us with terror and amazement, but we could not have believed the doctrine.[49]

* * * * *

Subject and Comment: **Cartloads of Trumpery**

194

Adams: Spent an hour in the beginning of the evening at Major Gardiner's where it was thought that the design of Christianity was not to make men good riddle-solvers, or good mystery-mongers, but good men, good magistrates, and good subjects, good husbands and good wives, good parents, and good children, good masters and good servants. The following questions may be answered some time or other, namely — Where do we find precepts in the Gospel requiring Ecclesiastical Synods? Convocations? Councils? Decrees? Creeds? Confessions? Oaths? Subscriptions? and whole cartloads of other trumpery that we find religion encumbered with in these days?[50]

* * * * *

Subject and Comment: **Ficticious Miracles**

Adams: The question before the human race is, whether the God of Nature shall govern the world by his own laws, or whether priests and kings shall rule it by fictitious miracles? Or, in other words, whether authority is originally in the people? or whether it has descended for 1,800 years in a succession of popes and bishops, or brought down from heaven by the Holy Ghost in the form of a dove, in a phial of holy oil?[51]

* * * * *

195

Subject and Comment: **Rack, Wheel, Fire, and Poker**

Adams: We think outselves possessed, or, at least, we boast that we are so, of liberty of conscience on all subjects, and of the right of free inquiry and private judgment in all cases, and yet how far are we from these exalted privileges in fact. There exists, I believe, throughout the whole Christian world, a law which makes it blasphemy to deny, or to doubt the divine inspiration of all the books of the Old and New Testament, from Genesis to Revelations. In most countries of Europe it is punished by fire at the stake, or the rack, or the wheel. In England itself, it is punished by boring through the tongue with a red-hot poker.

In America it is not much better; even in our own Massachusetts, which I believe, upon the whole, is as temperate and moderate in religious zeal as most of the States, a law was made in the latter end of the last century, repealing the cruel punishments of the former laws, but substituting fine and imprisonment upon all those blasphemers upon any book of the Old Testament or New.

Now, what free inquiry, when a writer must surely encounter the risk of fine or imprisonment for adducing any agrument for investigation into the divine authority of those books? Who would run the risk of translating Dupuis? I cannot enlarge upon the subject, though I have it much at heart. I think such laws a great embarrassment, great obstructions to the improvement of the human mind. Books that cannot bear examination, certainly ought not to be established as divine inspiration by penal laws.

It is true, few persons appear desirous to put such laws into execution, and it is also true that some few persons are hardy enough to venture to depart from them. But as long as they continue in force as laws, the human mind must make an awkward and clumsy progress in its investigations. I wish they were repealed. The substance and essense of Christianity, as I understand it, is eternal and unchangable, and will bear examination forever, but it has been mixed with extraneous ingredients, which I think will not bear examination, they ought to be separated.[52]

* * * * *

[**Benjamin Franklin:** Influential delegate and peacemaker among the delegates to the Constitutional Convention. Suggested that Congress have prayer each day. Inventor, philosopher, and statesman.]

Subject and Comment: **Respect Them All**

Franklin: I had been religiously educated as a Presbyterian; and though some of the dogmas of that persuasion, such as the eternal decrees of God, election, reprobation, etc., appeared to me unintelligible, others doubtful, and I early absented myself from public assemblies of the sect, Sunday being my studing day, I never was without some religious principles. I never doubted, for instance, the existence of the Deity; that he made the world, and governed it by his Providence; that the most acceptable service of God was the doing good to man; that our souls are immortal; and that all crime will be punished, and virtue rewarded, either here or hereafter.[53]

* * * * *

Subject and Comment: **Benjamin Franklin Not Saved?**

Franklin: Some of Mr. Whitefield's enemies affected to suppose that he would apply these collections to his own private emolument; but I, who was intimately acquinted with him (being employed in printing his Sermons and Journals, etc.), never had the least suspicion of his integrity, but am to this day decidedly of opinion that he was in all his conduct a perfectly honest man; methinks my testimony in his favor ought to have more weight, as we had no religious connection. He used, indeed, sometimes to pray for my conversion, but never had the satisfaction of believing that his prayers were heard. Ours was a mere civil friendship, sincere on both sides, and lasted to his death.[54]

* * * * *

Subject and Comment: **One God. Teachings of Jesus Corrupted. All Sects Acceptable**

Franklin: Here is my creed. I believe in one God, Creator of the Universe. That He governs it by his providence. That he ought to be worshipped. That the most acceptable service we render Him is doing good to His other children. That the soul of man is immortal, and will be treated with justice in another life respecting its conduct in this. These I take to be the principal principles of all sound religion, and I regard them as you do in whatever sect I meet with them. As to Jesus of Nazareth, my opinion of whom you particularly desire, I think the system of morals and his religion, as he left them to us, the best the world ever saw or is likely to see; but I apprehend it has received various corrupt changes, and I have, with most of the present dissenters in England, some doubts as to his divinity; though it is a question I do not dogmatize upon, having never studied it, and think it needless to busy myself with it now, when I expect soon an opportunity of knowing the truth with less trouble. I see no harm, however, in it being believed, if that belief has the good consequence, as probably it has, of making his doctrines more respected and better observed; especially as I do not perceive that the Supreme [Being] takes it amiss, by distinguishing the unbelievers in his government of the world with any peculiar marks of his displeasure.[55]

* * * * *

Subject and Comment: **At Peace with all Sects**

Franklin: All sects here, and we have a great variety, have experienced my good will in assisting them with subscriptions for building their new places of worship; and, as I have never opposed their doctrines, I hope to go out of this world in peace with them all. . . .[56]

* * * * *

Subject and Comment: **United States Created for all Religions**

Franklin: And it being found inconvenient to assemble in the open air, subject to its inclemencies, the building of a house to meet in was no sooner proposed, and persons appointed to receive contributions, but sufficient sums were soon received to procure the ground and erect the building, which was one hundred feet long and seventy broad, about the size of Westminster Hall; and the work was carried on with such spirit as to be finished in much shorter time than could have been expected. Both house and ground were vested in trustees, expressly for the use of any preacher of any religious persuasion who might desire to say something to the people of Philadelphia; the design in building not being to accommodate any particular sect, but the inhabitants in general; so that even if the Mufti of

200

Constantinople were to send a missionary to preach Mohammedanism to us, he would find a pulpit at his service.[57]

* * * * *

[**James Madison:** One of the authors of *The Federalist* papers. Called by historians the "Father of the Constitution" Fourth President of the United States.]

Subject and Comment: **Religious Persecution in America**

Madison: If the Church of England had been the established and general religion in all the northern colonies as it has been among us here, and uninterrupted tranquility had prevailed throughout the continent, it is clear to me that slavery and subjection might and would have been gradually insinuated among us. Union of religious sentiments begets a surprising confidence, and ecclesiastical establishments tend to great ingnorance and corruption; all of which facilitate the execution of mischievious projects.

I want again to breathe your free air. I expect it will mend my constitution and confirm my principles. I have indeed as good an atmosphere at home as the climate will allow; but have nothing to brag of as to the state and liberty of my country. Poverty and luxury prevail among all sorts; pride, ignorance, and knavery among the priesthood, and vice and wickedness among the laity. This is bad enough, but it is not the worst I have to tell you. That diabolical, hell-conceived principle of persecution rages among some; and to their eternal infamy, the clergy can furnish their quota of imps for such business. This vexes me the worst of anything whatever. There are at this time in the adjacent country not less than five or six well-meaning men in close jail for publishing their religious sentiments, which in the main are very orthodox. I have neither patience to hear, talk, or think of anything relative to this matter; for I have squabbled and scolded, abused and ridiculed, so long about it to little purpose, that I am without common patience. So I must beg you to pity me, and pray for liberty of conscience to all.[58]

* * * * *

Subject and Comment: **The Need for Freedom of Religion**

Madison: Who does not see that the same authority which can establish Christianity, in exclusion of all other Religions, may establish with the same ease any particular sect of Christians, in exclusion of all other Sects? That the same authority which can force a citizen to contribute three pence only of his property for the support of any one establishment, may force him to conform to any other establishment in all cases whatsoever?[59]

* * * * *

If "all men are by nature equally free and independent," all men are to be considered as entering into Society on equal conditions; as relinquishing no more, and therefore retaining no less, one than another, of their natural rights. Above all are they to be considered as retaining an "equal title to the free exercise of Religion according to the dictates of conscience." While we assert for ourselves a freedom to embrace, to profess, and to observe the Religion which we believe to be of divine origin, we cannot deny an equal freedom to those whose minds have not yet yielded to the evidence which has convinced us.[60]

* * * * *

Rulers who wished to subvert the public liberty may have found an established clergy convenient auxiliaries. A just government, instituted to secure and perpetuate it, needs them not. Such a government will be best supported by protecting every citizen in the enjoyment of his Religion with the same equal hand which protects his person and his property; by neither invading the equal rights of any Sect, nor suffering any Sect to invade those of another.[61]

* * * * *

Because, finally, "the equal rights of every citizen to the free exercise of his Religion according to the dictates of conscience" is held by the same tenure with all our other rights. If we recur to its origin, it is equally the gift of nature; if we weigh its importance, it cannot be less dear to us; if we consult the Declaration of those rights which pertain to the good people of Virginia, as the "basis and foundation of Government," it is enumerated with equal solemnity, or rather studied emphasis. Either then, we must say, that the will of the Legislature is the only measure of their authority; and that in the plenitude of this authority, they may sweep away all our fundamental rights; or, that they are bound to leave this particular right untouched and sacred: Either we must say, that they may control the freedom of the press, may abolish the trial by jury, may swallow up the Executive and Judiciary Powers of the State; nay that they may despoil us our very right to suffrage, and erect themselves into an independent and hereditary assembly: or we must say, that they have no authority to enact into law the Bill under consideration. We the subscribers say, that the General Assembly of this Commonwealth have no such authority: And that no effort may be omitted on our part against so dangerous an usurpation, we oppose to it, this remonstrance; earnestly praying, as we are in duty bound, that the Supreme Law giver of the Universe, by illuminating those to whom it is addressed, may on the one hand, turn their councils from every act which would affront his holy prerogative, or violate the trust committed to them: and on the other, guide them into every measure which may be worthy of his [blessing may re]dound to their own praise, and may establish more firmly the liberties, the prosperity, and the Happiness of the Commonwealth.[62]

* * * * *

Subject and Comment: **Religious Freedom**

Madison: Fortunately for this commonwealth, a majority of the people are decidedly against any exclusive establishment — I believe it to be so in the other states. There is not a shadow of a right in the general government to intermeddle with religion. Its least interference with it, would be a most flagrant usurpation. I can appeal to my uniform conduct on this subject, that I have warmly supported religious freedom.[63]

* * * * *

Subject and Comment: **Which Word is the Word?**

Madison: What edition; Hebrew, Septuagint, or Vulgate: What copy, what translation?

What books canonical, what apocryphal? The papists holding to be the former what protestants the latter, the Lutherans the latter what the protestants & papists ye former.

In what light are they to be viewed, as dictated every letter by inspiration, or the essential parts only? Or the matter in general not the words?[64]

* * * * *

Subject and Comment: **All Denominations Equal Under the Law**

Madison: I have received your letter of the 7th inst. with the Discourse delivered at the Consecration of the Hebrew Synagogue at Savannah, for which you will please to accept my thinks.[65]

* * * * *

Among the features peculiar to the Political system of the United States, is the perfect equality of rights which it secures to every religious Sect.[66]

* * * * *

Equal laws protecting equal rights, are found as they ought to be presumed, the best guarantee of loyalty and love of country; as well as best calculated to cherish that mutual respect and good will of every religious denomination which are necessary to social harmony and most favorable to the advancement of the truth.[67]

Notes

1. Norman Cousins, *In God We Trust,* (New York: Harpers & Brothers, 1958), pp. 173-216.

2. Supra, pp. 21-23.

3. Supra, pp. 395-396. From *The Age of Reason.*

4. Supra, p. 432. From *Prospect Papers.*

5. Supra.

6. Supra, p. 433.

7. Supra, p. 438-440.

8. Supra, pp. 393-394.

9. Supra, 401.

10. Supra.

11. Letter to Thomas Erskine, September, 1797. See: Cousins, supra, p. 405.

12. Supra, p. 409.

13. Supra, p. 410.

14. Supra.

15. Supra, p. 413.

16. Cousins, supra, p. 418.

17. Note 2, p. 429.

18. Note 2. p. 430.

19. Letter to Bishop Moore. See: Cousins, supra, p. 437.

20. Jefferson's notes on the Religious Freedom Act of 1786. See: Cousins, supra, pp. 121-123.

21. From Jefferson's autobiography, begun in 1821. See: Cousins, supra, p. 120.

22. Letter to James Madison, December 16, 1786. See: Cousins, supra, p. 121.

23. Letter to Joseph Priestly, March 21, 1801. See: Cousins, supra, p. 131.

24. Letter to Danbury Baptist Association, January 1, 1802. See: Cousins, supra, p. 135.

25, Letter to William Short, April 13, 1820. See: Cousins, supra, p. 151.

26. Letter to Thomas Whittemore, June 5, 1822. See: Cousins, supra, p. 158.

27. Letter to nephew, Peter Carr, August 10, 1787. See: Cousins, supra, pp. 128-129.

28 Letter to William Fishback, September 27, 1809. See: Cousins, supra, p. 138.

29. Letter to Samuel Kercheval, January 19, 1810. See: Cousins, supra, p. 139.

30. Letter to William Camby, September 18, 1813. See: Cousins, supra, p. 140.

31 Letter to Miles King, September 26, 1814. See: Cousins, supra, pp. 144-145.

32. Letter to Exra Stiles, June 25, 1819. See: Cousins, supra, p. 148.

33. Letter to William Short, April 13, 1820. Cousins, supra, p. 150.

34. Letter to William Short, August 4, 1820. See: Cousins, supra, pp. 152-153.

35. Letter to William Pickering, February 27, 1821. See: Cousins, supra, p. 157.

36. Letter to Thomas Cooper, November, 2, 1822. See: Cousins, supra, p. 163.

37. Letter to Joseph Priestly, April 9, 1803. See: Cousins, supra, p. 166.

38. Letter to Benjamin Rush. See: Cousins, supra, p. 117.

39. Letter to John Adams, April 11, 1823. See: Cousins, supra, p. 291.

40. Letter to Mrs. Harrison Smith, August 6, 1816. See: Cousins, supra, p. 147.

41. Letter to John Adams, August 1, 1816. See: Cousins, supra, p. 278.

42. Letter to Hebrew congregation of Newport, 1790. See: Cousins, supra, p. 61.

43. Letter to Baltimore church, January 27, 1793. See Cousins, supra, p. 62.

444 Letter to Sir Edward Newenham, June 22, 1792. Cousins, supra, p. 67.

45. Letter to Richard Cranch, October 18, 1756. See: Cousins, supra, p. 93.

46. Letter to F.A. Van Der Kemp, December 27, 1816. See: Cousins, supra, pp. 104-105.

47. Letter to John Tyler, 1814. See: Cousins, supra, pp. 106-107.

48 Letter to Thomas Jefferson, July 9, 1813. See: Cousins, supra, p. 232.

49. Letter to Thomas Jefferson, September 14, 1813. See: Cousins, supra, p. 239.

50. The diary of John Adams, February 18, 1756. See Cousins, supra, p. 80.

51. Letter to Thomas Jefferson, June 20, 1815. See: Cousins, supra, pp. 264-265.

52. Letter to Thomas Jefferson, January 23, 1825. See: Cousins, supra, p. 293.

53. Franklin's autobiography. See: Cousins, supra, p. 25.

54. Franklin's autobiography. See: Cousins, supra, p. 38.

55. Letter to Ezra Stiles, March 9, 1790. See: Cousins, supra, p. 42.

56. Supra, p. 43.

57 Franklin's autobiography. See Cousins, supra, p. 37.

58. Letter to William Bardford, Jr., January 24, 1774. See: Cousins, supra, p. 299.

59. *Memorial and Remonstrance*, 1785. See: Cousins, supra, p. 310.

60. Supra, p. 310.

61. Supra, pp. 311-312.

62. Supra, pp. 313-314.

63. Madison's journals, June 12, 1788. See: Cousins, pp. 314-315.

64. Madison's notes, 1784. See: Cousins, supra, p. 303.

65. Letter to Jacob D. La Motta, August, 1820. See Cousins, supra, p. 320.

66. Ibid.

67. Note 64, pp. 320-321.

APPENDIX

Index to Editor's *Subjects and Comments* with Quotations of the Founding Fathers

INDEX